INDIA
1947-1997
New Light on the Indus Civlization

INDIA
1947-1997
New Light on the Indus Civlization

B.B. Lal

Aryan Books International
New Delhi

INDIA—1947-1997
New Light on the Indus Civlization

ISBN: 978-81-7305-129-6

First Published: 1998

Reprinted: 2023

Published by:

Aryan Books International
Pooja Apartments, 4B, Ansari Road, New Delhi-110002 (India)
Tel.: 23287589, 23255799; Fax: 91-11-23270385
E-mail: aryanbooks@gmail.com
www.aryanbooks.com

Printed in India

In the Golden Jubilee Year
of India's Independence,
this book is dedicated
to all those
who are not professionals,
yet have an enlightened interest
in India's past

CONTENTS

PREFACE

In January this year—the fiftieth year of India's Independence—came out my book, *The Earliest Civilization of South Asia*. It appears to have been well received by the scholarly community, both in India and abroad, although, as might be expected, it has also generated debate on some of the topics contained therein. This is very healthy and I gratefully welcome it. However, a section of the intelligentsia, after going through the book, confided to me that it was a bit too detailed and somewhat too tough for the average enlightened reader interested in India's past. Such a reader, they told me, would have been happier if a simpler book was produced on the subject, highlighting more specifically the manner in which explorations and excavations in post-Partition India have added to our knowledge of this great civilization of South Asia. It is more or less in response to this demand that the present book is being brought out. May it be hoped that it meets the need.

August 15, 1997 **B.B. Lal**

ACKNOWLEDGEMENTS

As usual, Shri Krishna Deva has been kind enough to go through the text and make valuable sugestions. To him I am ever grateful. My eldest son, Air Commodore Rajesh Lal, was given some chapters to read in order to assess how a lay reader reacts to the presentation. Thanking him would be a formality, but I must say that his reactions have been useful. He has also been good enough to read the proofs, in which job Shri Vishnu Kant too has assisted.

Excavations at Dholavira are still on and there is quite a lot which has not yet come in print. Shri R.S. Bisht, the excavator, has been kind enough to make available to me some unpublished data, for which I am greatly beholden to him. My thanks are also due to Shri Raj Nath Kaw for many of the photographs published herein and to Shri S.K. Sharma and Shri Vishnu Kant for the drawings. My daughter-in-law, Sushama Lal, has made the conjectural paintings of Dholavira reservoir and draw-well, and, as always, my wife, Kusum, has been of great help at various stages. A young member of the family, my grandson Nikhil ('the Golfer', as he would like to be addressed), has helped me in preparing the Index. To all of them I am greatly indebted.

Last but not least, I wish to thank Shri Vikas Arya for taking personal interest in publishing the book.

LIST OF ILLUSTRATIONS

A. FIGURES

B. COLOUR PLATES

CHAPTER I

FROM DARKNESS TO LIGHT. ONCE AGAIN DARKNESS, BUT THIS TIME FOLLOWED BY MUCH BRIGHTER LIGHT

As late as the early decades of this century it was believed that there did not exist any civilization worth the name on the Indian subcontinent prior to the invasion of Alexander in 326 BC. This was the view held by almost all the western historians in spite of the fact that it was well known that there did exist the *Veda*s which, even on a very conservative (though arbitrary) estimate of Max Muller, were at least as old as 1200 BC.

However, in the early years of the third decade, an altogether new vista was thrown open. Two eminent Indian archaeologists, namely Daya Ram Sahni and R.D. Banerjee, carried out trial excavations, the former at Harappa in 1921 and the latter at Mohenjo-daro in 1922, bringing to light material remains which pushed with a single stroke the antiquity of civilization on the Indian subcontinent from the third century BC to the third millennium BC. Subsequent large-scale excavations, at Mohenjo-daro by John Marshall and his colleagues (Marshall 1931) and at Harappa by M.S. Vats (1940), revealed a detailed picture of this civilization which in many ways excelled the other contemporary civilizations, viz. those of the Nile valley in Egypt and the Tigris-Euphrates valleys in Iraq.

The most outstanding feature of this civilization was the planning of its urban centres. Usually, the settlement was divided into two parts, loosely called the 'Citadel' and the 'Lower Town,' with a system of fortifications which differed from site to site. While the former contained within it some monumental buildings, the latter enclosed habitational houses in general. The streets in the latter were normally oriented along the cardinal directions, thus producing a gridiron pattern. Care was also taken to provide a good drainage system, either by laying underground drains through the streets or by installing soakage jars immediately outside the houses, which evidently were regularly cleaned up.

The houses were made of either kiln-fired or sun-dried bricks, but the interesting point is that these were manufactured in a set ratio of 4:2:1 (40 x 20 x 10 cm or 30 x 15 x 7.5 cm), which enabled the masons to build the walls in alternate courses of headers and stretchers, a technique that gave them the necessary strength.

While the mainstay of the Harappan economy was agriculture, in which wheat and barley played dominant role, there is ample evidence of a variety of crafts having been practised by the Harappans, such as copper-smithery, lapidary, shell-working, pottery-making, etc. No less noteworthy was the art of producing excellent sculptures in stone as well as in metal, for who is there who does not hold his/her breath while having a look at the famous 'dancing girl' in bronze from Mohenjo-daro? But one must take hats off to craftmen who cut the superb steatite seals which bear exquisitely engraved human and animal figures. Indeed, the majestic bull with its prominent horns and hump and a swinging dewlap must have been the envy of any contemporary craftman the world over.

The Harappans had a monumental script which appears on their seals, sealings, metallic objects, pottery, etc. Some read a Dravidian language in it, while others a kind of proto-Sanskrit. Some even go to the extent of reading whole Vedic verses in certain seals. The hard fact, however, remains that no one has hit the mark.

The Harappans were engaged in internal as well as external trade. The latter is fully attested to by the discovery of seals, sealings, weights, etched carnelian beads and other objects of Harappan origin in countries known today as Iraq, Bahrain, Oman, Iran and Turkmenia. In fact, the Harappans themselves had an exclusive settlement of their own in north-eastern Afghanistan, viz. that at Shortughai.

Unfortunately, sometimes facts are stranger than fiction. The very river, viz. the Indus, from which India derived its name, is no longer within its bounds. With the partition of the country in 1947, not only did the Indus pass on to Pakistan but, along with it, also the sites of the civilization that acquired its name from that river, viz. the Indus Civilization. Only two very insignificant sites, viz. Kotla Nihang in Panjab and Rangpur in Gujarat remained within the Indian border, and even their 'Indusness' was debated (fig. 1.1).

Such was the state of affairs in 1947. Indian archaeologists, however, accepted the challenge and by 1984 (Joshi et al. 1984) placed on the map of present-day India as many as 800 sites associated with various stages of that civilization. (The search is still on and the number would be much more now.) This number, incidentally, is greater than that of such sites discovered so far in Pakistan. It must also be stressed that this civilization extended far beyond the Indus valley—right into the upper Gaṅgā-Yamunā *Doāb* in the north and to as far south as the upper reaches of the Godāvarī in Maharashtra (fig. 1.2). Indeed, some scholars have argued that, on the basis of such a far-flung distribution of its remains, it is no longer justified to call it the "Indus" Civilization. They have used a new name—the Indus-Sarasvatī Civilization (e.g. Gupta 1996). But this one too is not free from criticism, since, as already mentioned, the civilization extended as far south as Maharashtra. To strike a compromise, it may be better to use another name, viz. Harappan Civilization, already given to it after the name of the site where it was first discovered. In the present book, however, the prevalent names have been used without any differentiation.

Let it be stressed that it is neither the number nor the extent that matters. What does matter is that the Indian discoveries have added altogether new dimensions to our knowledge of this great civilization of the third millennium BC. Thus, for example, Kalibangan, in Rajasthan, has brought to light the earliest agricultural field, dating back to ca. 2800 BC and associated with a cultural milieu that preceded and contributed to the make-up of the Mature Stage of the Indus Civilization itself. The same site has given evidence of the earliest earthquake ever revealed through an excavation, dating back to ca. 2600 BC. Lothal, in Gujarat, has given to the Indus Civilization the earliest dockyard. Located in the same State, Dholavira has shown that the settlement

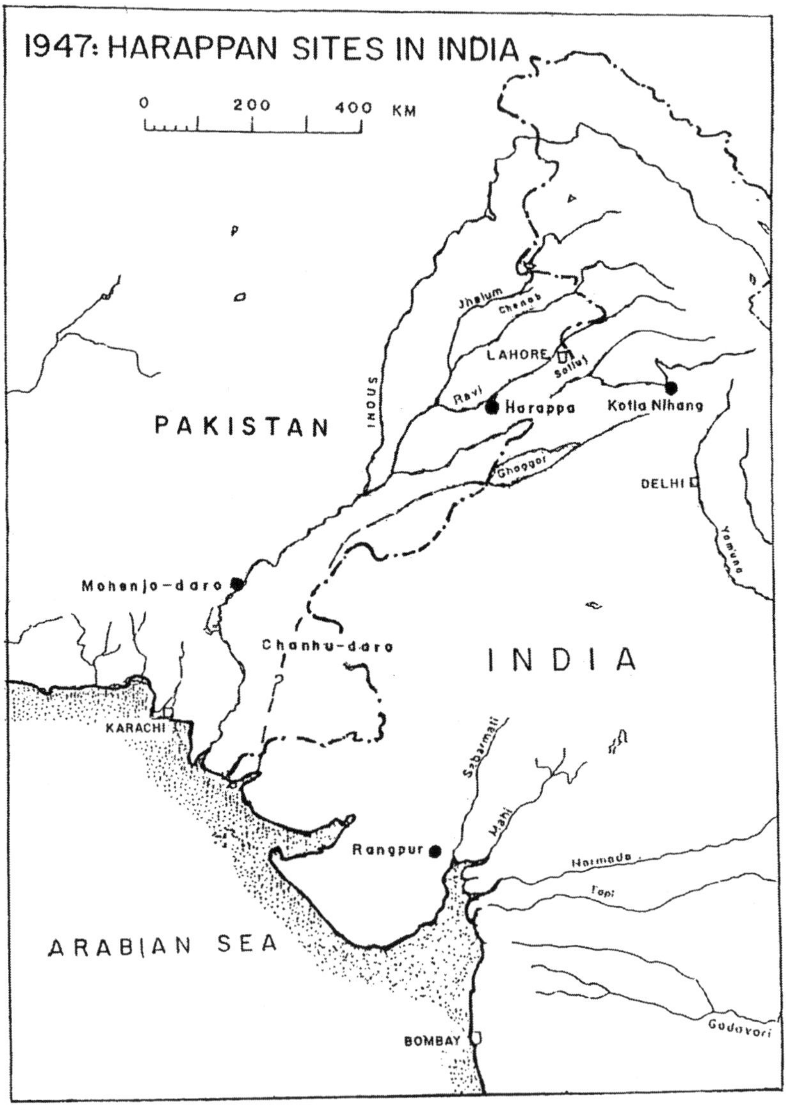

Fig. 1.1 **1947**: Harappan sites in India

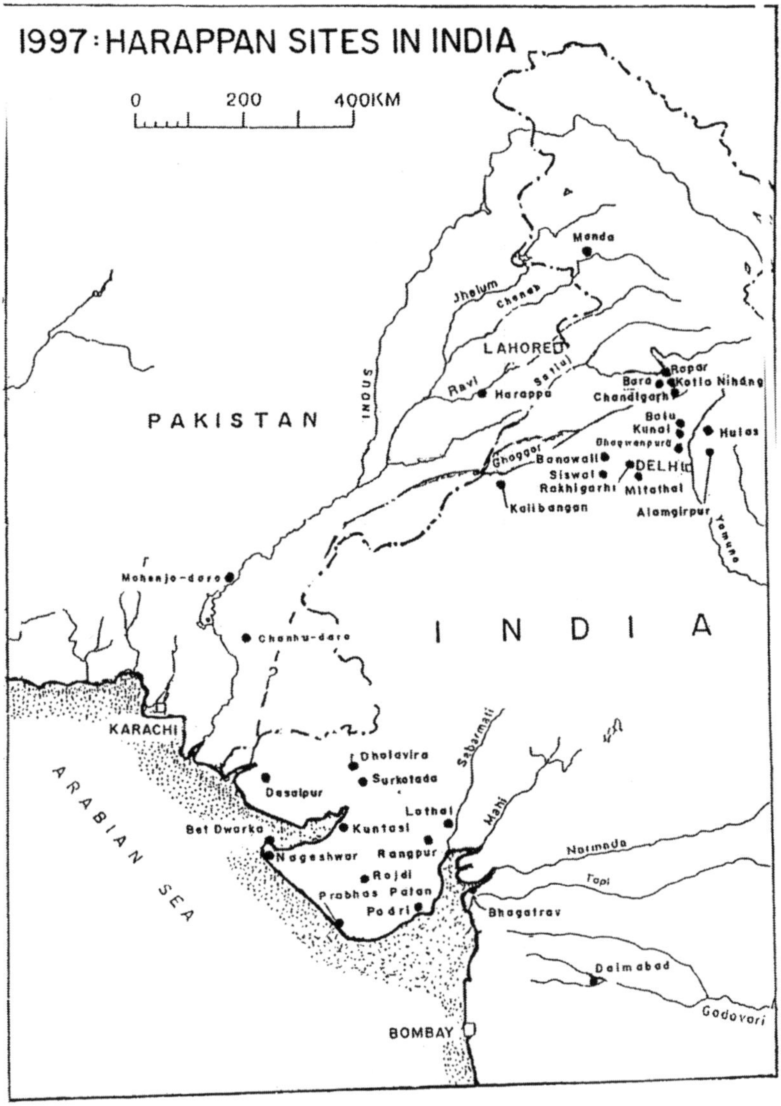

Fig. 1.2 **1997**: Harappan sites in India

was divided into three parts—a 'Citadel,' a 'Middle Town' and a 'Lower Town.' This site has also yielded very interesting evidence regarding water-management.

Excavations have also thrown new light on the religion of the Indus people as well as on their burial practices. Contrary to the general belief that this civilization was destroyed by invading Aryans, it is now clear that there was no such destruction, much less by the Aryans. Instead, there was a decline of the civilization due to several factors, such as the drying of certain rivers, climatic changes, wearing out the landscape and, last but not least, a steep fall in trade, particularly external. In due course, the cities gave way to villages, but the latter did carry down with them a good deal of non-urban Harappan legacy.

The book seeks to highlight these and other new features of the Indus Civilization revealed on the extra-Indus territory, i.e. within the domain of India.

CHAPTER II

THE INDUS CIVILIZATION WAS NOT BUILT IN A DAY: THE TALE OF ITS EVOLUTION

As mentioned earlier, explorations and excavations carried out in India since Independence have not only revealed new facets of the Indus Civilization but have also thrown valuable light on a cultural milieu that preceded its Mature Stage and, in the course of time, gave rise to the latter. This evidence comes from a number of sites in Haryana and Rajasthan, located along the now-dry courses of rivers amongst which particular mention may be made of the Sarasvatī, Dṛisadvatī and Ghaggar. Palaeogeographical evidence shows that in antiquity these streams combinedly constituted a mighty river, which, as the literary evidence suggests, went by the name of the Sarasvatī—a river so much eulogized in the Vedic texts. Its immense size is duly confirmed by the vast stretch of its bed even now, though dry. We shall deal here with only three of the sites located on this river-system, viz. Kunal, Kalibangan and Banawali.

Situated in district Hissar, Haryana, Kunal is remarkable in a number of ways, though it covers only a small area, viz. about 1.2 hectares (Khatri and Acharya 1995). With a vertical deposit of a little over 3 m, the occupational strata are divisible into three subperiods, called Ia, Ib and Ic, from bottom upwards.

Since the land was somewhat undulating, the first settlers at the site levelled it up with a red kankary soil brought from the neighbourhood. At the levelled surface they dug circular pits, about a metre in depth and 2 m in diameter. Along the edges of these pits post-holes have been noted, indicating that these otherwise shallow pits were supplemented with some kind of a wattle-and-daub superstructure to make them habitable. Since we have yet to discover the ancestors of the first inhabitants of Kunal, we do not know if the first Kunalians inherited the so-called 'pit-dwelling' tradition from them. Anyway, pit-dwelling was a feature in many parts of the ancient world and hence the Kunal evidence need not surprise us. Living partially below the surrounding ground-level may have perhaps provided some succour from the cold winter winds.

Anyway, these first Kunalians had fully stepped into what is known as the chalcolithic stage of cultural evolution, i.e. when metal had come to be used though stone and bone tools were not given up. The metal used was copper of which arrow-heads and fish-hooks have been found. These were evidently used for hunting and fishing. Micro-beads of chalcedony also deserve to be noted in the cultural repertoire. However, the most noteworthy component was the pottery. It comprised a red ware bearing painted designs in two colours: usually with a black outline filled in with white. Such pottery is characteristic of a number of sites along the Sarasvatī valley, both in India and in the adjacent area in Pakistan, known as Cholistan. These early levels of Kunal have also yielded potsherds in what has come to be known as the Hakra Ware from a type-site in Cholistan. As of today, this is the earliest pottery known in the Sarasvatī valley.

By Subperiod Ib the size of the pit-huts increased, ranging between 2.64 m and 2.92 m in diameter. The pits were also now lined with mud bricks. Cooking was done inside the huts, as indicated by mud-brick hearths on the floors. The bichrome pottery of the earlier Subperiod occurred in greater abundance but the 'Hakra Ware' dwindled. Amongst the painted motifs special mention may be made of the peacock and pipal-leaf (pl. IA) which, it may be stated, are amongst the more noteworthy designs of the Mature Harappan Stage. Alongside there also occurred beakers and jars in sturdy red ware forecasting the typical Mature Harappan Ware. To cap it all, there were the terracotta 'cakes' which, again, become characteristic of the Mature phase.

The transition towards the Mature Stage became more and more apparent as time passed. Thus, in Subperiod Ic not only did the pit-huts give way to square or rectangular houses but bricks of the typical Harappan ratio, viz. 4:2:1, also came to be manufactured. Grain-production seems to have increased, as indicated by the construction of circular silos, plastered with a mixture of lime and clay.

That the Kunalians were really getting prosperous is clearly evidenced by the recovery of jewellery and other associated material from two of the houses. There lay buried in one of them a globular jar of red ware which contained silver ornaments wrapped in a silver sheet. These comprised 'two tiaras, one small and one large, each with a large fully opened flower having petals topped with a decoration like the Greek letter alpha' (Khatri and Acharya 1995: 86; here pl. IIA). Along with these tiaras there also occurred a multi-spiralled armlet (pl. IB), reminding us of a similar armlet worn by the famous dancing girl from Mohenjo-daro (pl. IC). In the other house have been found a large number of gold/silver beads: cup-shaped, barrel-shaped, discular, etc. Most of these shapes continue in the Mature Harappan Stage. For example, discular beads with perforation along the diameter (pl. IIB) are quite the same as those found in the Mature levels at Lothal (pl. IIC). There also occurred in other parts of the site beads of lapis lazuli, carnelian, faience, which are significant in one way or another.

That copper objects were being produced at the site is clearly indicated by the discovery of a terracotta crucible with molten metal still sticking to it. The objects included axes, fish-hooks, spearheads, inverted 'V'-shaped arrow-heads, coiled cones and coiled finger-rings, most of which remind us of their Mature Harappan counterparts.

Though small in size, the settlement at Kunal brings out certain aspects very clearly. In the first place, it was in trade-contact with other parts of the country and even outside it, since materials like copper, silver and lapis lazuli had to be brought from elsewhere. While copper may have come from the Khetri mines which continued to be exploited by the Mature Harappans as well, lapis lazuli had no source within an easy reach: it had to come all the way from the hilly areas west of the Indus—Afghanistan or Baluchistan. We do not know from where the Kunalians got their silver. It may well be that they were not the direct importers. In that case, one has to visualize a network of trade-mechanism.

In the context of trade one must draw attention to the discovery from the site of seven seals, six of steatite and one of shell. These are square in shape and are provided with a perforated knob at the back, just as in the case of their Mature Harappan counterparts. The only, though noteworthy, difference between these and the Mature ones is that the former bear only geometric but no animal motifs, much less the distinctive inscriptions. Though some graffiti have been reported from Kunal, a regular system of writing still remains the high-water mark of the Mature stage, as do weights and measures.

Although not much evidence could be gleaned regarding any social stratification from the limited excavations at Kunal, the discovery of the silver tiaras, along with other precious objects would tend to show that a few families were much richer than others. Further, if the tiaras are taken to have been used as in later days, namely by the royalties or 'some one in particular', then one might well argue that there were some people who were socially at a much higher level than the rest. Maybe here we have a case for a chief or a politico-religious head.

Lastly, a word about the chronological horizon of the site. Three radiocarbon dates place it between ca. 3016 and 2577 BC (Calib-3 calibration, 1 Sigma; cf. Lal 1997, p.84). It is, therefore, abundantly clear that the archaeological milieu at Kunal, which represents a formative stage of the Mature Harappan Civilization, is also consistent chronologically. (While a somewhat detailed analysis of the evidence regarding the dating of the Mature Stage of the Harappan Civilization would be given in a subsequent chapter, here it may suffice to state that the beginning of the Mature Stage is assignable to ca. 2600 BC.)

About 20 km from Kunal, as the crow flies, is the site of Banawali which is better known for its Mature Harappan remains (Chapter III) but which has also yielded valuable evidence in regard to both Early and Late Harappan times.

Because of the thick overlying deposits of the Mature Harappan stage not much area of the Early/Formative stage could be excavated. All the same, some very useful information could be gathered, particularly about the town-planning. Whereas Kunal did not yield any evidence of a fortification surrounding the settlement, Banawali did. In fact, even within the lifetime of the Early Period, there did come up the concept of a twofold division of the settlement, namely a 'Citadel' and a 'Lower Town,' which became quite characteristic of the subsequent Mature Harappan times.

Within the total thickness of about 3 m of the Early Period, three subperiods have been identified on the basis of structures and associated material. From bottom upwards, these have been labelled as IA, IB and IC.

Right from the beginning of the settlement, the houses were oriented along the cardinal directions, thus allowing the streets to run east-west and north-south, a typical Mature Harappan feature. However, the bricks used in Subperiod IA were in the ratio of 3:2:1 (30 x 20 x 10 cm), which is un-Harappan. As evidenced by Kalibangan also, this perhaps was the more prevalent ratio during the Early Harappan times in the Sarasvatī valley. It was in Subperiod IB that the fortification wall was constructed. Even today it stands to a height of about 2 m, and has a basal width of 3.6 m.

The pottery used in Subperiods IA and IB was characteristically similar to that found at Kalibangan, to be dealt with in some detail a little later.

Subperiod IC yielded evidence which entitles it to be called 'transitional' between the Early and Mature Harappan. To quote the excavator, R.S. Bisht (*Indian Archaeology 1986-87—A Review*, p.33), this Subperiod is to be noted for 'drastic and diagnostic changes in architecture, planning and antiquities in an otherwise continuing milieu of the preceding Subperiod. The entire settlement was planned and constructed *de novo*. The dichotomous layout which the Harappans adopted was introduced during this Subperiod. The fortification of the previous period [Subperiod] was externally chiselled or partially sliced away and doubled in width for housing the citadel, and the lower town was laid out contiguously towards the east as well as the north, while the position in the west remained unresolved.' It may also be noted that the typical Harappan ratio of brick-size, viz. 4:2:1, also came up during this Subperiod, while bricks in the earlier ratio of 3:2:1 also continued to be manufactured. It has generally been assumed that the Early Harappans did not fire their bricks. This impression is belied by the evidence from Banawali, where fired bricks were used in the construction of some of the houses.

In pottery, besides the earlier ones, a ware with red slip and having certain typical Mature Harappan shapes also appeared in Subperiod IC. Also to be noted are terracotta 'cakes' and chert blades, both, again, associated with the Mature Harappan stage. Without any break, the occupation passed on to Period II which had all the characteristics of the Mature Harappan times and with which we shall deal in Chapter III.

Proceeding about 120 km straight south-west from Banawali, one comes to the site of Kalibangan, located along the left bank of the Ghaggar, in Hanumangarh District of Rajasthan. There are two major parts of the settlement, a relatively smaller one on the west and a larger one on the east (see fig. 3.1). The overall perimeter is about 1.5-2 km, and the maximum height about 10 m.

While the eastern part was occupied only during Mature Harappan times, it is the western part that has both Early and Mature remains. However, because of the thick deposits of the Mature stage, only a limited area of the Early Period (I) could be exposed. Nevertheless, the plan and other details of the fortifications were duly obtained (fig. 2.1). The fortification-walls formed a rough parallelogram, the longer axis being almost north-south. While the eastern side measured 250 m, the western was a little less and also deflected a little to the west. The result was that whereas the southern side measured only 170 m, the stretch of the northern was much larger. In the north-western part of the northern side, an entrance was also located, which had some interesting features. After running for about 115 m from its eastern end, the northern wall turned south-westwards for 45 m. Through this arm was provided the entrance. Thereafter there was another arm, turning west-north-west, which joined the northern end of the western wall. Such an arrangement for locating the entrance is noteworthy, since any attack on the settlement or even an unauthorized entry into it could have been duly thwarted by the inhabitants by positioning themselves on the in-turned arms and counter-attacking the intruder, from two sides. In this context, it may also be stated that this entrance faced the river and was thus more vulnerable.

The houses inside were also oriented along the cardinal directions (fig. 2.2), with the result that the streets and lanes ran north-south and east-west. The walls were constructed with sun-dried bricks. However, kiln-fired bricks were also used, in drains where there was direct contact with water. These bricks were un-Harappan in their ratio, which was 3:2:1. There is

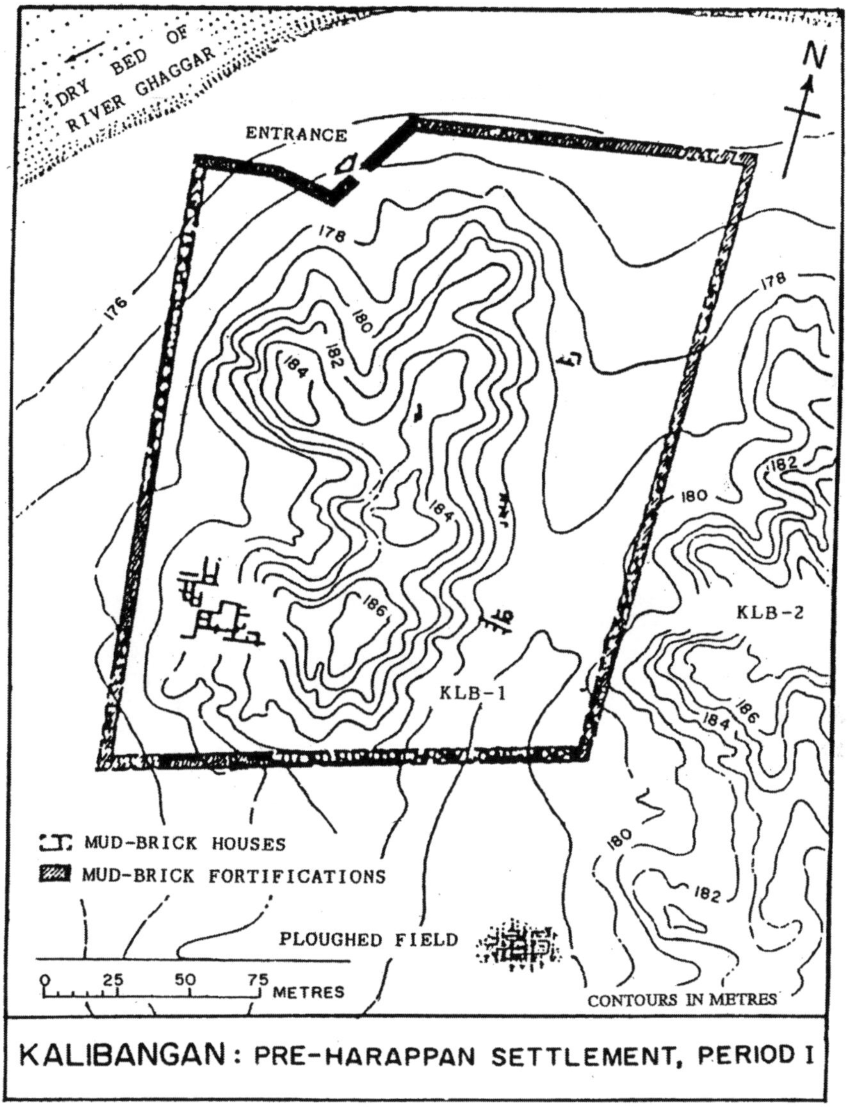

Fig. 2.1 Kalibangan: Pre-Harappan settlement, Period I

Fig. 2.2 Kalibangan: Early Harappan structures

evidence of plastering the walls. The houses usually had a courtyard with rooms on the sides. Within the courtyard were noted wide circular pits, plastered with lime and mud. These appear to have been used for storage of grains, though no actual cereals were found. Cooking was also done in the courtyard, as evidenced by the presence of *tandūrs*. These were of both overground and underground varieties (fig. 2.3). This discovery throws the antiquity of modern *tandūrs* back into the first half of the third millennium BC.

A very noteworthy discovery of this Early Harappan Period was that of an agricultural field to which we shall refer separately in detail (Chapter V). Here it may suffice to say that this is the earliest agricultural field ever

Fig. 2.3 Kalibangan: Early Harappan *tandūrs* (cooking ovens)

discovered through an excavation anywhere in the world.

The commonest pottery of this period was a red ware, usually without any slip but painted in two colours, namely black and white. This kind of pottery, it may be stated, was characteristic of the Early Harappan sites, not only in India but also in Pakistan. The most common amongst the painted designs were thick and thin bands in the upper part of the body. Besides the foregoing category of pottery, which has been classed as 'A', there were other five, called B-F. Of these, one may refer to another Early Harappan type (classed as D), viz. a sturdy red ware basin with deeply incised designs on the interior. Finally, mention must be made of pots under category C, which anticipated those of the subsequent Mature Harappan times, e.g. flanged-rim jars, dishes- and cups-on-stand. Made of fine-grained clay, carefully potted and well fired, these had a plum to red slip. The painted designs, usually executed in black pigment, included cross-hatched loops, fish-scales, filled-in triangles, metopes, etc. (fig. 2.4).

That the Early Harappan Kalibanganites were well within the Copper/Bronze Age is shown by the occurrence of a large number of tools and other objects in these metals, such as axes, bangles, etc., besides a *parasū*. This last-named item, it may be stated, is used even today in Rajasthan for cutting shrubs.

The Early Harappan settlement at Kalibangan came to an end because of an earthquake to which we shall refer in some detail later (Chapter VI).

The foregoing data from Kunal and from the early levels of Banawali and Kalibangan make it abundantly clear that there did exist in the Sarasvatī/Ghaggar valley a culture which had many features that were carried over to the subsequent Mature stage of the Harappan Civilization. To recapitulate, in the Early Harappan levels there is evidence of town-planning, i.e. of the laying out of the houses and consequently of the streets along the cardinal directions. There is also evidence of the settlement having been fortified. In fact, even the concept of a division of the settlement into two parts, namely a 'Citadel' and a 'Lower Town,' so characteristic of the Mature Harappan stage, had also come up (Banawali IC). Though the more favourite brick-ratio of the early settlers in this valley was 3:2:1, the typically Mature Harappan ratio of 4:2:1 also emerged soon. Again, though these Early Harappans were using mainly sun-dried bricks, it is also clear that they fired their bricks. In fact, not all the houses at all Mature Harappan sites were made of kiln-fired bricks. For example, the houses at Banawali, Kalibangan and Lothal were predominantly made of sun-dried bricks.

The Mature Harappan pottery is very distinctive—a sturdy red ware with typical designs painted in black colour. While the Early Harappan pottery is not so sturdy and is usually painted in two colours, viz. black and white, there is ample evidence to show that a sturdy red ware with paintings in black had begun to emerge towards the end of the Early stage. Some of the specific

Fig. 2.4 Kalibangan: Painted designs on Early Harappan pottery. Solid line or filling denotes black colour; hatching, white

shapes, e.g. dishes- and cups-on-stand, flanged jars, ring-stands, had also appeared and so also some of the characteristically Mature Harappan painted designs: pipal-leaves, peacocks, hatched triangles, fish-scales, etc. Even triangular terracotta 'cakes', diagnostic of the Mature Harappan times had begun to show up at some of the sites in the Early stage. Mention has earlier been made of discular beads of silver from Kunal, having perforation along the diameter, which are exactly similar to the gold ones from the Mature Harappan levels of Lothal.

But then there are also some noteworthy differences between the two stages. The Mature Harappan stage stands out because of its use of weights and measures, seals and sealings and a system of writing. Further, it is distinguished by the much larger size of its settlements, its monumental buildings and sculptural art in metal as well as stone. Thus, while granting that there did exist a base for the Harappan Civilization to grow upon, this quantum jump has got to be accounted for.

The weights and measures are clearly associated with trade and commerce. And similar seems to be the case with the seals which were evidently used for sealing the packages that were sent out. Likewise, writing may have become a necessity for adding the name of the consignee/consignor, as well as for maintaining records. Thus, a major spurt in trade, both internal as well as external, seems to have been at the root of the introduction of a system of weights and measures and of writing. In this context, it may be well worthwhile to recall that ca. 2600 BC, the approximate time of the rise of the Mature stage of the Harappan Civilization, is also the time when there began to occur a number of objects of Mature Harappan origin at several sites in Western Asia. A boost in trade must have led to economic prosperity, which in turn must have led to the rise of an elite class amongst the population, an expansion of the size of settlements, construction of monumental buildings and finally the production of a variety of objets d'art. Towards this boost in trade, rise in agricultural and industrial production (e.g. etched carnelian beads so ubiquitous in Western and Central Asia) and a back-up by the administrative authorities must have contributed a lot.

This then, in brief, is the tale of the emergence of a great civilization on the Indian subcontinent in the third millennium BC.

CHAPTER III

NO MONOTONY: EACH SETTLEMENT HAD ITS OWN PLANNING

It has been held for long that the Harappan Civilization was sadly monotonous, both in time and space, i.e. from the middle of the third millennium BC to the first quarter of the second and from Sutkagendor in Baluchistan (Pakistan) in the west to Alamgirpur in Uttar Pradesh (India) in the east. Recent researches, however, have shown that this was hardly the case. And here we shall take just five sites from amongst those excavated in India since Independence to illustrate the point. These are: Kalibangan, Banawali, Lothal, Surkotada and Dholavira.

(i) KALIBANGAN

As mentioned earlier, Kalibangan is situated on the left bank of the Ghaggar which is now dry but, judging from its wide bed, must have been a massive river in ancient times (then perhaps known as the Sarasvatī, as indicated by literary sources). With a perimeter of about 1.5-2 km, the site has three parts, from west to east. While the westernmost part has been labelled as the 'Citadel' and the central as the 'Lower Town,' the easternmost has not been given any special name. It contains a few ritualistic structures.

Unlike Mohenjo-daro where it is not yet clear whether the 'Lower Town' was fortified, the 'Lower Town' at Kalibangan has yielded clear evidence of having been duly fortified (Lal 1979). The fortifications formed a rough parallelogram on plan, the eastern and western walls running due north-south, but the northern one slightly deviating from east-west (fig. 3.1). Since the

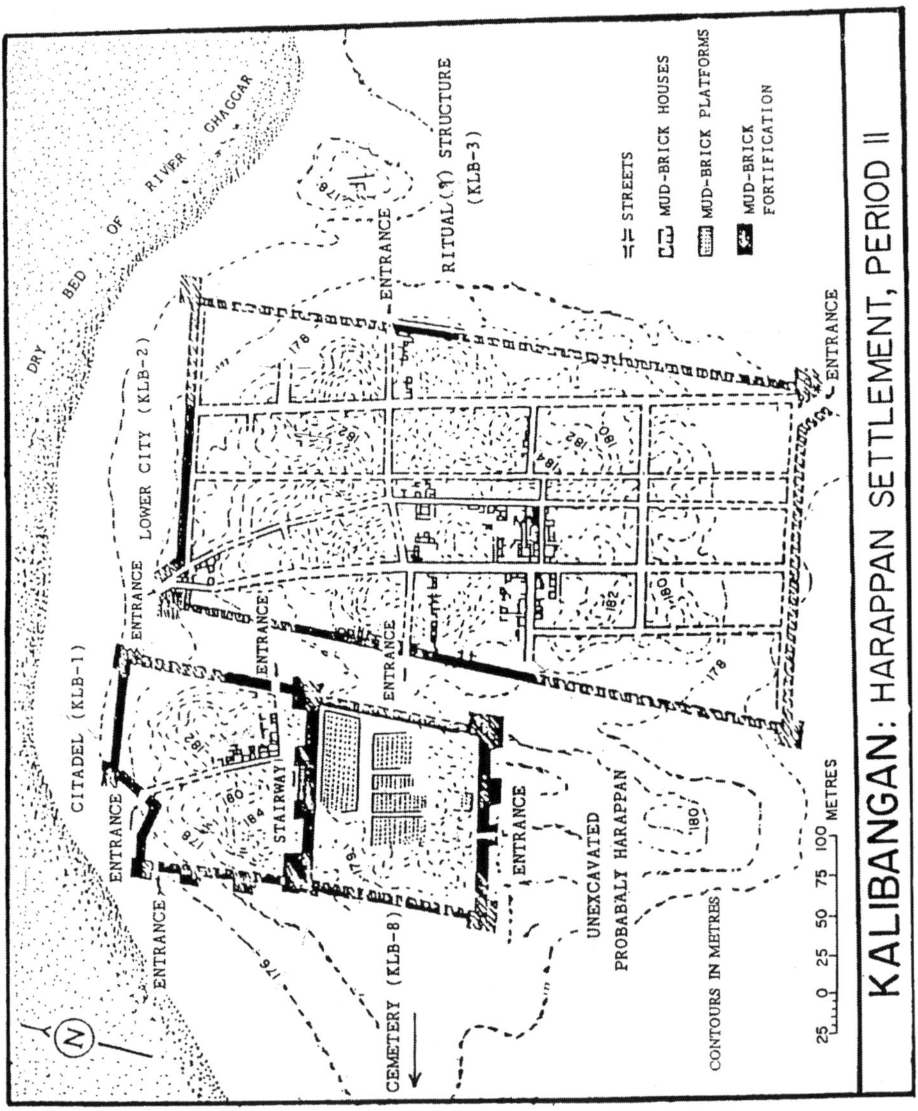

Fig. 3.1 Kalibangan: Harappan settlement, Period II

mound is eroded at the southern end, nothing definite can be said in respect of the southern wall. However, it may be assumed that the southern wall was parallel to the northern one.

While the east-west extent of the Lower Town was easily measurable—it was 240 m, indications are that the north-south distance was in the neighbourhood of 360 m. The fortification-walls were made of mud bricks, though at a few places kiln-fired bricks were also employed. To begin with, large-sized bricks (40 x 20 x 10 cm) were used but in subsequent repairs there were smaller ones (30 x 15 x 7.5 cm).

The settlement within was laid out more or less in a grid-pattern. While the longer streets did not quite follow the alignment of the north-south fortification-walls, the east-west streets, though often staggered, did follow the alignment of the northern wall. A very interesting point to be noted about the lanes and streets was that these fell in a ratio of 1:2:3:4. Thus, while the narrowest, evidently a lane, was 1.8 m in width, the others were 3.6 m, 5.4 m and 7.2 m respectively (figs. 3.2 and 3.3).

An average house had a courtyard with rooms along its three sides and an entrance on the fourth. The entrance was sufficiently wide, so as to let a bullock-cart in. In the courtyard there were rectangular troughs, made of mud bricks, for placing therein fodder for the cattle. Also, the lower parts of large jars were embedded in the ground for providing water. Cooking was also usually done in the courtyard, wherein a well was also sometimes located.

The rooms were often paved with mud bricks and sometimes even with decorated tiles. But attention must be drawn to a special technique adopted by the builders. They first put a soling of terracotta nodules intermixed with pieces of charcoal. Over it was laid the clay floor. This process was repeated when renewing the floor (fig. 3.4). It was not easy for us to understand the reason for this kind of arrangement. We then consulted the local engineers who told us the secret. They said that this practice of laying a soling of nodules intermixed with charcoal was followed even now in many villages. The purpose of intermixing charcoal pieces is twofold. In the first place, it prevents moisture from travelling upwards along the walls—a problem often faced in mud houses. Secondly, it acts as anti-termite. Should not the Kalibanganites be given

Fig. 3.2 Kalibangan: The widest (7.2 m) street in the Lower Town

full credit for their ingenuity?

While the rooms were used for different purposes, such as sleeping, storage, etc., it appears that one was reserved for ritualistic purposes. In it have been noted what have been called 'fire-altars' in the absence of a better name. More will be said about these fire-altars when we deal with new light on Harappan religion (Chapter XII). However, these are not to be confused with the fire-altars of the Parsis.

It needs to be emphasized that the civic authorities were very particular

Fig. 3.3 Kalibangan: Another street in the Lower Town

Fig. 3.4 Kalibangan: Successive floors of clay with soling of terracotta nodules and charcoal, Lower Town

about not allowing any encroachment on the streets. Throughout the nine or so structural reconstructions that Kalibangan witnessed, from about 2600 BC to about 1900 BC, not a single structure intruded on the street. The only structures that were noted on the sides of the streets were small platforms adjacent to the entrances to the respective houses. These were a part of the approved plan, and in no way encroachments. In this context, it would be interesting to mention that even now the villages and small towns in this area have such platforms immediately outside the entrance, where the occupants of the house and neighbours sit and chat.

Located about 40 m to the west of the Lower Town, the Citadel had its

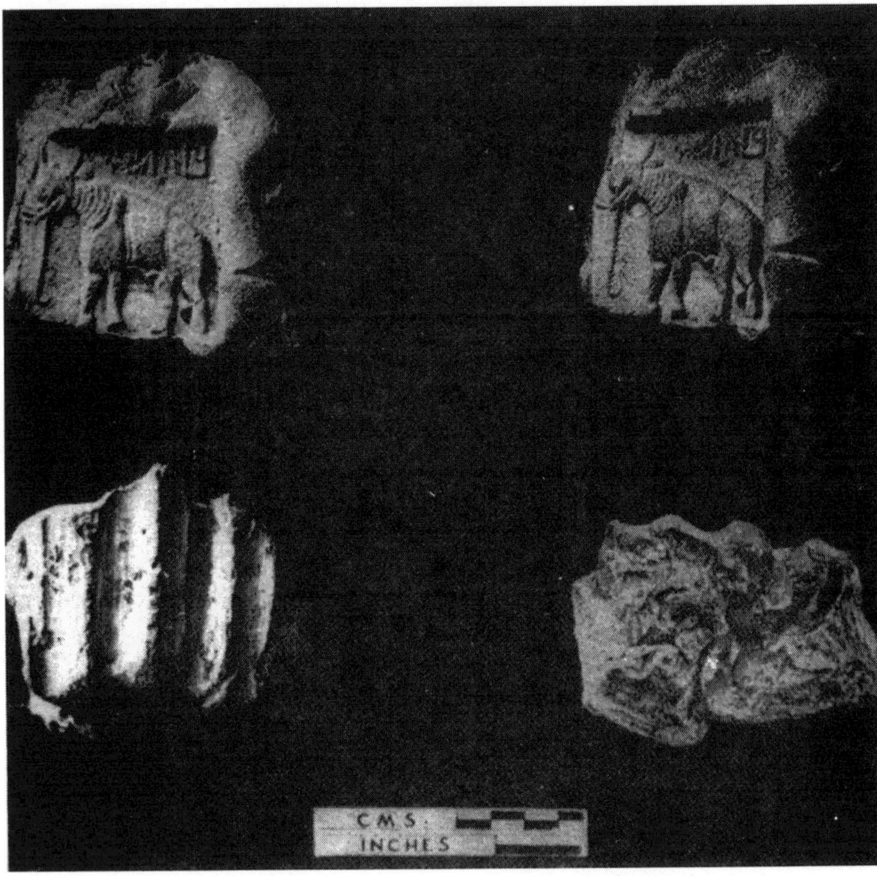

Fig. 3.5 Kalibangan: Four views of a clay sealing bearing impressions of seals, reeds and knotted thread

own fortification-system. Forming a parallelogram on plan, 240 m north-south and 120 m east-west, the complex was divided into two equal rhombs by a partition-wall in the middle (fig. 3.1). While in the northern rhomb there were residential houses located on each side of a street running up to a gateway in the north-west, the southern rhomb did not have any such houses. Instead, it contained a series of cardinally oriented mud-brick platforms, separated one from the other as also from the fortification-walls. Owing to the ravages of time and man, most of the superstructures on these platforms have disappeared, but at least in two cases it was possible to identify the nature of what once stood there. On one there was a 'fire-altar' complex, while on the other a sacrificial pit. To both these we shall refer when we deal with new light that excavations in India have thrown on the Indus religion (Chapter XII).

We have already referred to an entrance to the northern rhomb, located at the north-western end. There was another gate in the south-eastern part of this rhomb, providing access to the occupants of the Lower Town which had its own gate a little to the south of this one.

There were two entrances also to the southern rhomb: one from the northern rhomb and the other from the area south of the southern rhomb itself. The former pierced through the medial partition-wall, and was provided with mud-brick steps. That on the southern side lay across the southern wall and also had an elaborate passageway built in a stepped fashion. Thus, an interesting point that needs to be noted is that whereas the two entrances to the northern rhomb, being on a level ground, allowed vehicular traffic to get in, those to the southern rhomb, because of their stepped nature, did not. This difference seems to be quite in consonance with the nature of the two rhombs, the northern having residential buildings, but the southern containing religious structures located on high platforms. Evidently, it must have been thought pertinent that those entering the southern rhomb for performing religious rites should move on foot and not keep on riding about in vehicles.

The Harappan levels of Kalibangan have yielded some very interesting antiquities. For example, besides the typical square seals, there was a cylindrical one (pl. IVA) which points to Mesopotamian influence, since cylindrical seals were common there but rare in the Harappan milieu. There are some sealings which throw valuable light on how the seals were used. For example, fig. 3.5 shows four different views of one and the same sealing of clay. In the lower row may be seen the impressions of reeds of which the package was made as also of the knotted thread. The upper row shows impressions of the seals. The process thus can be reconstructed as follows.

The commodity concerned was placed in a package of reed or some similar material. The package was then tied with a thread or rope, as necessary. Finally, a lump of clay was placed over the knot and the clay was stamped with the seal of the sender or senders as the case may be.

Amongst the terracotta objects attention may be drawn to a *kernos* with seven lamps affixed to it (pl. IVB). It is not unlikely that it was used on some ceremonial occasions and carried about on the head. Two bulls, one each in terracotta and bronze (pls. IIIA and IIIB), are remarkable for their vigorous execution.

(ii) BANAWALI

Some 120 km to the north-east of Kalibangan lies the site of Banawali, in Hissar District, Haryana. To its south is the dry bed of a river which may have been the Sarasvatī itself, though now it finishes off some distance up in the north-east. The ancient remains cover an area measuring approximately 400 x 400 m, roughly oriented north-south and east-west. The occupational deposits, about 8 m in thickness, are divisible into three periods, numbered I, II and III from bottom upwards. We have already referred to Period I, which is Early Harappan. Period II is Mature Harappan, while III is post-Mature Harappan.

The Mature Harappan town-plan at Banawali is quite different from what we saw at Kalibangan. Here the settlement was not divided into separate units. Instead, the entire complex lay within a single fortified area. However, within this area the Citadel too had its own fortifications (fig. 3.6). Thus, while the Citadel partook of a common wall with the Lower Town on the southern side, it had its own fortification-walls on the other sides, forming roughly a semi-ellipse on plan. The thickness of these walls varied from 5.4 to 7 m. Beyond these walls, on the northern, eastern and to some extent on the western side as well, there was the Lower Town, having its own fortification-walls and forming a rough quadrangle on plan.

Not a very wide area inside the Citadel could be excavated, yet it was clear that in it there were houses and adjoining streets, roughly oriented along the cardinal directions. Whether the Citadel contained platforms also, bearing

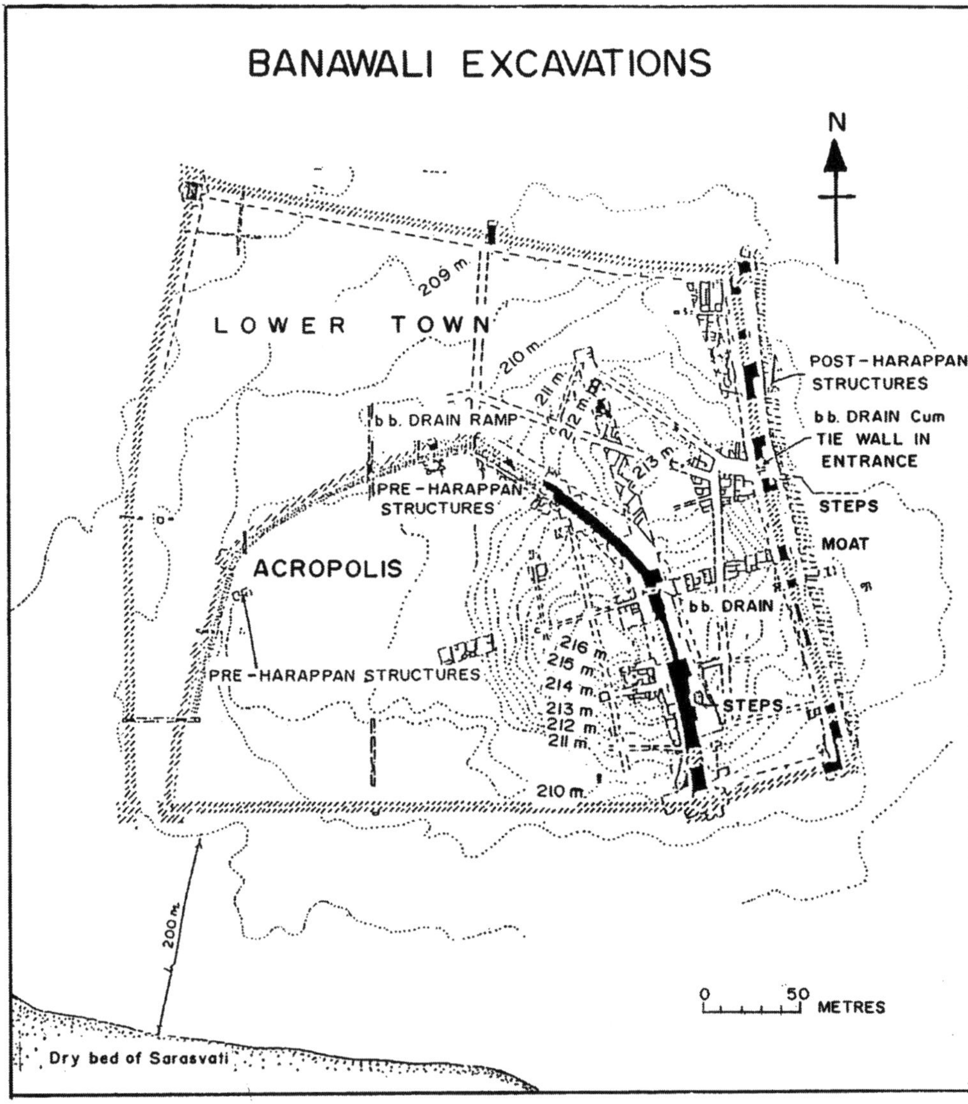

Fig. 3.6 Banawali excavations

Fig. 3.7 Banawali: Section across the moat, Period II

some specialized structures, as at Kalibangan, could not be determined. There was a narrow opening in the eastern wall of the Citadel, through which passed a drain. It is not certain if this opening also acted as a passageway. However, on the exterior at this point there was a square bastion, there also being another further to the south. Roughly at the apex of the ellipse there was a 1.5-m wide ramp, paved with kiln-fired bricks, which did provide an interconnection between the Citadel and the Lower Town.

The layout of the Lower Town too did not follow the classic grid-pattern. Instead, its streets ran in all directions. Thus, while a street, emanating from the above-mentioned ramp did run south-north, a street forking from it ran in an east-south-east direction. This street joined three other streets, running in various directions, at a piazza close to an entrance through the eastern fortification-wall of the Lower Town. This wall too was provided on the exterior with square bastions at intervals. However, the most noteworthy feature of the Banawali fortifications was the provision of a moat, which was identified on the exterior of the eastern wall (fig. 3.7). As regards the supply of water to the moat, there was the river, hardly 200 m to the south. The water would have easily been inducted from the upper reaches of the river, carried through the moat and finally discharged back into the river. However, because of lack of extensive excavations the moat could not be traced around the entire periphery. Anyway, the provision of a moat does really add another new dimension to the fortification-system of the Harappans.

An average house in the Lower Town followed the usual pattern of having a courtyard with rooms on sides. Some of the houses, however, were large and seem to have belonged to well-to-do persons. For example, one of the houses yielded many seals and weights and may have belonged to a merchant. Further, its toilet 'was provided with a wash basin placed on a high place in a corner near the drain which carried off the waste water into a sullage jar placed ouside on the street' (Bisht 1982: 117). Another big house yielded weights and a large number of beads variously of carnelian, lapis lazuli and gold. However, very interesting was the discovery of 'a touchstone bearing gold streaks of different hues', indicating that the practice of testing gold, as used even now, is as old as 4,500 years.

(iii) LOTHAL

Located at a distance of about 80 km south-east of Ahmedabad in Gujarat, Lothal, as mentioned earlier, has given to the world the earliest dockyard. Though today there is no active river in the vicinity of Lothal, there is enough evidence to show that anciently there was one. This river met the Bhogāvo which, in turn, joined the Sābarmatī, the main river of the region. The Sābarmatī falls in the Gulf of Khambhat which is an inlet of the Arabian Sea. Thus, a clear link between Lothal and the sea was established. While we shall turn to the details of this dockyard in Chapter VII, here we shall deal with the general layout of the settlement which, once again, is different from that of all other

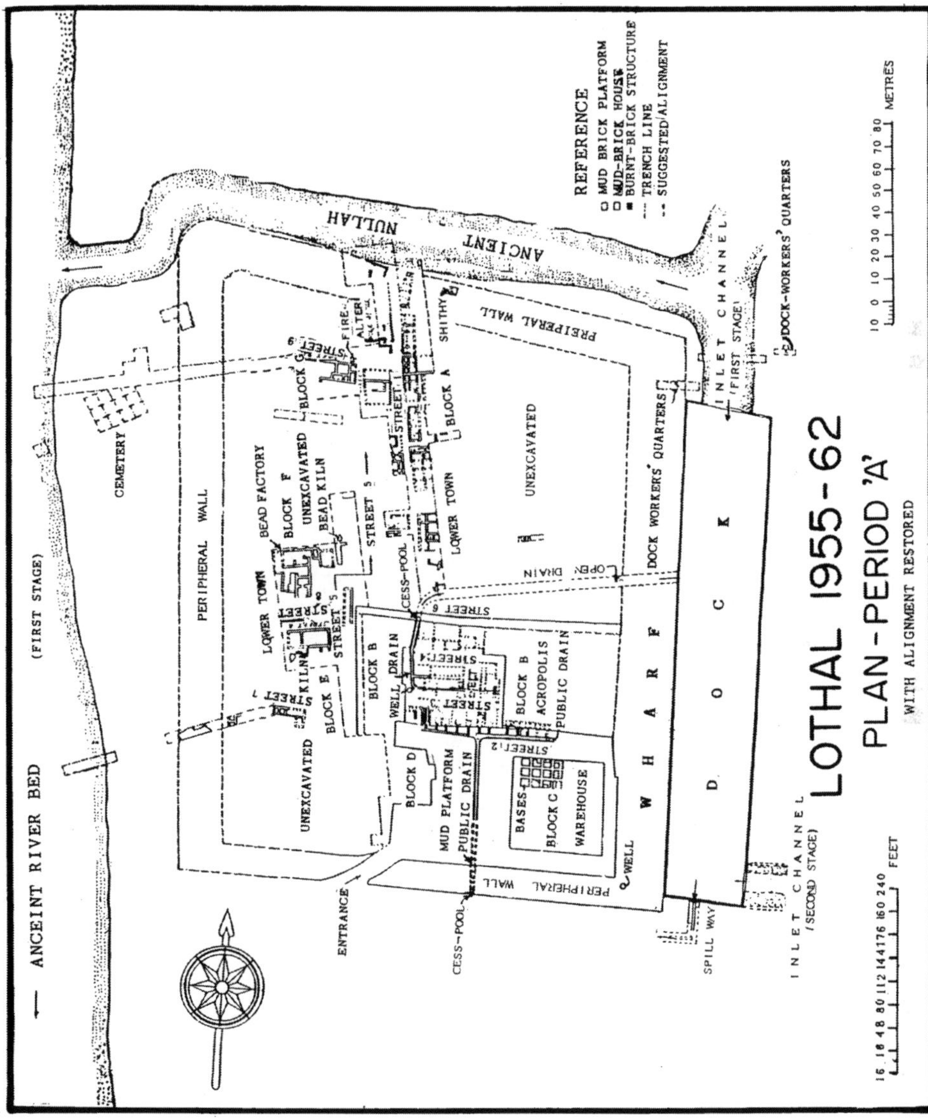

Fig. 3.8 Lothal: Plan, Period 'A'

Fig. 3.9 Lothal: Bathing pavements and drains in the Acropolis

sites including Kalibangan and Banawali.

Oriented along the cardinal directions and forming a rough rectangle on plan, the fortified settlement measures about 225 m east-west and 280 m north-south (fig. 3.8). There is, however, evidence to indicate that a section of the population also dwelt outside the fortified area. The fortification-wall, made

Fig. 3.10 Lothal: Kiln for bead-making

essentially of mud but reinforced at places with mud bricks, had an average thickness of about 12-13 m. The eastern side, against which the dockyard was located, however, measured much more—about 20-21 m in width—since at least a part of it seems to have functioned as a wharf. It has survived to a height varying between 1.8 m and 2.4 m.

Though lying within the overall fortified area, the Citadel or the Acropolis (as called by the excavator: Rao 1979 and 1985), did not have a fortification-wall of its own, as did the Citadel at Banawali. Nevertheless, it had its own identity and separateness, having been built on a raised platform in an exclusive area in the south-east. The platform, with a core of mud and veneer of mud bricks, was roughly trapezoidal on plan, the eastern and western sides

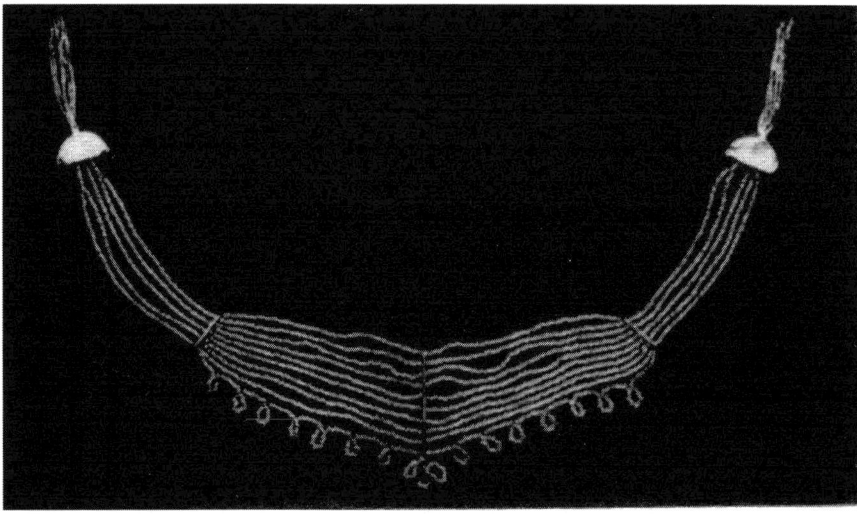

Fig. 3.11 Lothal: Micro-beads of gold

measuring about 118 m each and the southern and northern ones, respectively 113 m and 125 m. The height of this platform was about 3.5 m. On it there stood some residential buildings, with the streets/lanes running north-south and east-west. However, mention must also be made of a complex comprising a set of twelve bath-pavements with accompanying drains (fig. 3.9). Since much of what originally stood there has disappeared because of ravages of time, it is difficult to visualize the function of this unit of twelve bathing pavements. However, if it is justified to project the Kalibangan evidence on Lothal, it is not unlikely that these pavements may have had some kind of ritualistic association, as certainly was the case with the Kalibangan well, bathing platform and drain, all located close to a group of seven fire-altars (Chapter XII).

To the south of the aforesaid structures there was a major complex which has been identified as a warehouse. With it we shall deal in detail when we discuss the dockyard (Chapter VII).

Piercing the southern fotification-wall there was an entrance. If there were others these have remained unexplored. Anyway, a lot has been opened up

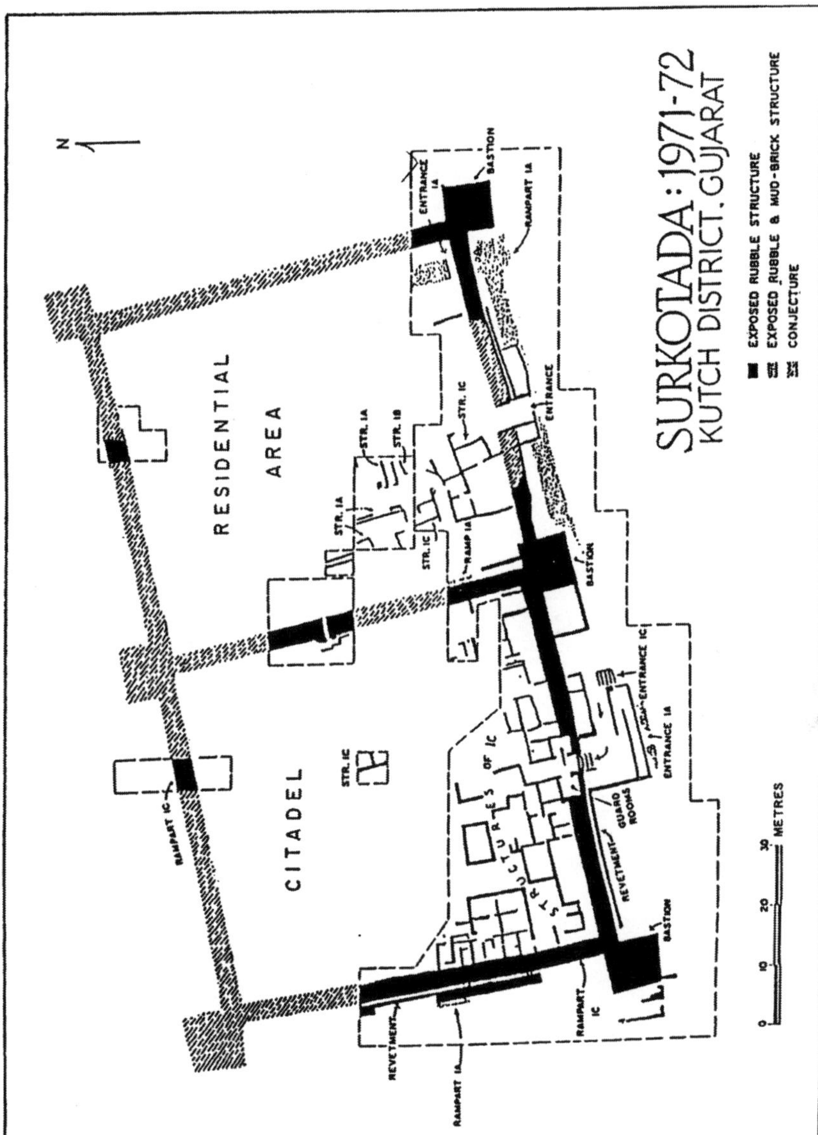

Fig. 3.12 Surkotada: General layout

in the Lower Town where many criss-cross streets, running north-south and east-west, have been recorded. While the widest one measured 12 m across, the narrowest was about 3.6 m. One of the streets, designated as the Bazar Street, had a number of shops along its sides.

The houses were on the usual pattern, with a courtyard surrounded by living rooms. In many houses 'fire-altars' have also been identified. Some of the houses have yielded copper ingots, crucibles, etc. showing that these belonged to coppersmiths. Likewise, the discovery of raw material, lots of beads in various stages of manufacture and even a kiln (fig. 3.10) shows that the occupant must have been a bead-manufacturer. In this context it may be well worth mentioning that etched carnelian beads of Harappan origin have been found at a number of sites in contemporary Iraq, Persian Gulf, Iran and Central Asia. In fact, this part of Gujarat even today specializes in the manufacture and export of beads.

Within a total of about 8.5 m of occupational deposits, two main Periods have been identified, called A and B, from bottom upwards. While Period A has four phases, numbered I-IV, Period B has only one, Phase V. Phase I marks just the beginning of the settlement, but it was in Phase II that the township took its shape. Phase III represents the peak, whereafter a decline began to set in, culminating in Phase V.

The Harappan levels of Lothal have yielded a number of important objects which include seals, sealings, a variety of copper objects, gold jewellery (fig. 3.11 and pl. IIC), an ivory scale, an angle-measuring instrument and, last but not least, a terracotta horse the significance of which will be discussed later (Chapter XV).

To the west of the settlement, a cemetery has been identified in which at least three graves have yielded two skeletons each. To these we shall refer when we take up the various modes of the disposal of the dead by the Harappans (Chapter XIV).

(iv) SURKOTADA

As already mentioned, almost each urban Harappan settlement had its individualistic plan. Thus, Surkotada, located 160 km north-east of Bhuj in Kachchha, was no exception (Joshi 1990). It had both the components, viz. a Citadel and a Lower Town, but with a difference. In its case the two parts were juxtaposed, with a common wall in between, an opening through which provided access from one to the other (fig. 3.12). Further, there was no appreciable difference between their sizes: each one, a rough square on plan, measured about 60-65 m internally. The orientation, however, was as usual, viz. along the cardinal directions, the combined longer axis being approximately east-west. Roughly about the middle of the southern wall of both the Citadel and the Lower Town, there was a gateway. However, whereas the one leading into the Lower Town was a simple affair, the entrance to the Citadel was elaborate. This latter was provided with a ramp, barbican, steps and guard rooms. The provision of steps would mean that no vehicular traffic could get into the Citadel, a situation similar to that in the southern part of the Citadel at Kalibangan. There was another difference between the Citadel and the Lower Town. Whereas the structures in the former are reported to have been built over platforms, that was not the case in the Lower Town.

Constructed right at the beginning of the occupation, the fortification-wall had a 7-m thick core of mud and mud bricks, provided with veneer of stone rubble. There is also evidence of mud plaster having been applied to it. As is to be expected, it underwent repairs from time to time.

It is not very clear if these two squares constituted the entire settlement at the site. If indeed there was no other area under occupation in the immediate neighbourhood, then certainly Surkotada cannot be regarded as a settlement on the lines of other sites like Kalibangan, Lothal, etc. In that case, was there any special reason for this small yet fortified establishment? Had we enough evidence about the war-equipment of the Harappans, we would have taken Surkotada as a garrison town. That being not the case, was it some kind of a trading outpost or an administrative centre? The question begs an answer.

In all, three occupational subperiods, called IA, IB and IC, were identified. That there was no pre-Mature Harappan occupation at the site is indicated by the presence of a typical Harappan seal even in Subperiod IA. At the same time the occurrence of the pointed bottom goblet, which is usually associated with a latish phase of the Harappan Civilization, would indicate that it was not right at the beginning of the Mature Phase that Surkotada came into existence. The end of Subperiod IB is marked by some kind of conflagration. Was it in any way associated with the arrival of a new people using a white-painted black-and-red ware, whose original domain was in southern Rajasthan?

To the south-west of the fortified area, a cemetery has been identified. It has yielded some unusual types of burials. We shall deal with them when we take up the Harappan burials in detail (Chapter XIV).

(v) DHOLAVIRA

Located on one of the islands in the Rann of Kachchha, Dholavira is indeed outstanding amongst the sites of the Harappan Civilization (Bisht 1989 and 1991). Not only has it yielded a unique town-plan, but it has also brought to light a remarkable system of water-supply. The discovery over here of the only stadium known to the Harappans is yet another feather in the cap of the Dholavirans. And they can very well be proud of producing the largest ever Harappan inscription, as also polished stone pillars which no other Harappan site has.

Before we take up the layout and other details of the site, it may be well worthwhile to have a brief look at the cultural evolution and subsequent devolution over here. The approximately 12-m-thick vertical deposits have been divided into seven stages. Of these, Stages I and II may be regarded as being somewhat anterior to the Mature Harappan Phase, though during these many of the would-be Mature Harappan elements had begun to manifest themselves. For example, the mud bricks had the usual Harappan ratio of 4:2:1, the pottery included dishes-on-stand and perforated jars, and even the characteristic terracotta 'cakes' were there. By Stage III most of the typical Harappan pottery-forms, weights and seals made their appearance, although the seals bore only the animal figures, without the usual inscription. Stage IV, with a deposit of about 5.5 m, represents the Mature Harappan Civilization in its full bloom. The seals now had inscriptions as well. And to this stage may also be assigned the large inscription and polished stone pillars. In Stage V a kind of devolution began to set in: for example, loss of civic control over

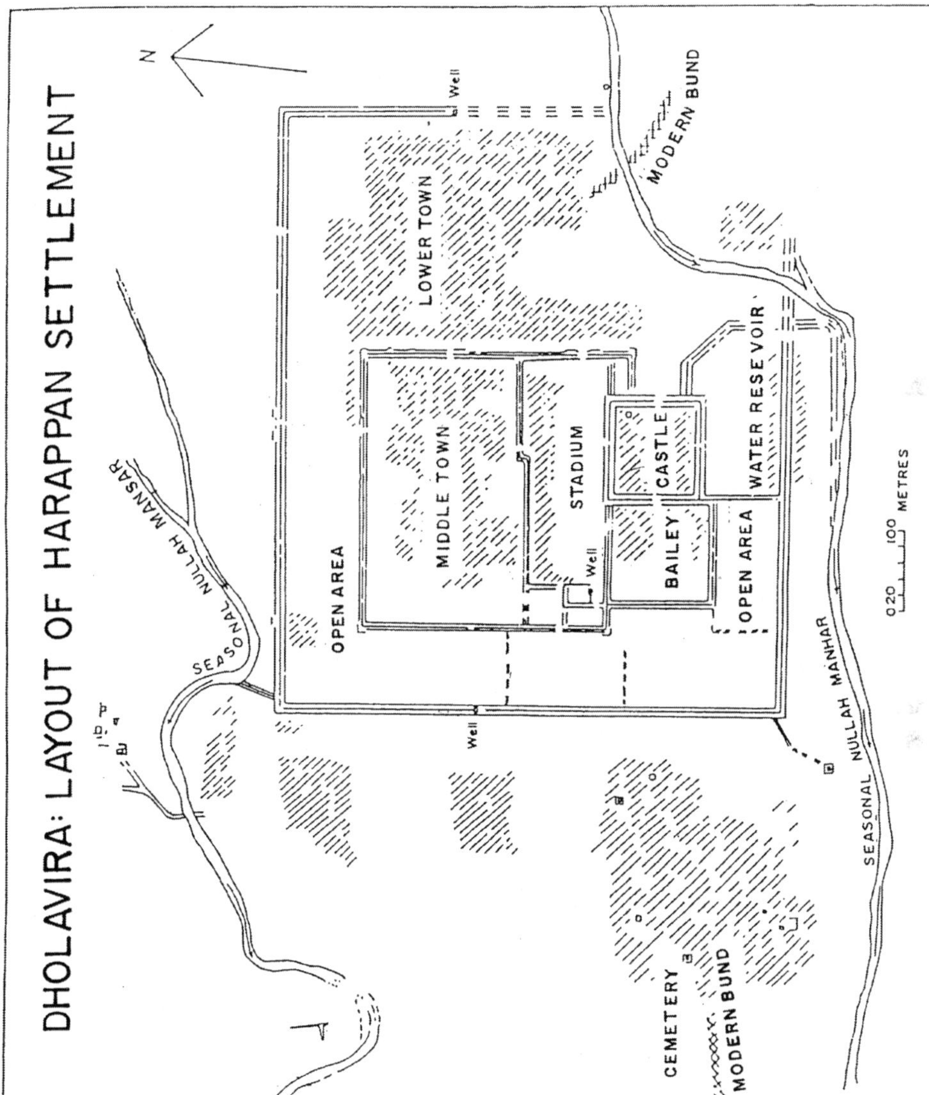

Fig. 3.13 Dholavira: Layout of Harappan settlement

the layout and maintenace of structures. At this point, the site was also deserted for a while.

In Stage VI, when the site was reoccupied, some more changes were visible. Thus, while many of the Harappan pottery-forms continued, a black-and-red ware also appeared. The layout of the houses also changed and the size of the settlement diminished. Further, while the typical Harappan weights continued, the seals were now bereft of the figures. There was once again a desertion. However, when the site came under occupation for the last time (Stage VII), the houses showed an altogether different pattern. These were now small and circular. There was no town-plan, not to speak of a drainage system. In spite of all these changes, the similarity of many of the pottery-forms and other artefacts between Stages VI and VII indicates that it was just a case of cultural devolution.

In the above brief survey we have casually referred to some of the antiquities found at Dholavira. However, particular attention needs to be drawn to two stone sculptures, since stone sculptures are rare at Harappan sites in India. One of these is a seated human figure, 38 cm in height. The head is missing. Both the legs are bent. The left hand rests on the left knee. The right hand is broken. But what is of particular interest is the probable presence of the *ūrdhva-liṅga* (upraised male organ). The relevant portion is highly abraded and therefore one cannot be too sure of this particular feature. At the same time, the possibility cannot also be ruled out. If this feature did really exist, the figure would recall to mind the famous Paśupatī seal from Mohenjo-daro, where the deity does have an *ūrdhva-liṅga*. In such an event, the Dholavira figure too may have been of some deity.

The other figure is very likely that of a mongoose. It is pretty large, 37 cm in length. Needless to add that it has been very nicely carved.

Now to the layout. Although the remains of ancient habitation extend even outside the fortified area, the latter, forming a rectangle on plan and oriented along the cardinal directions, measures approximately 770 m east-west and 615 m north-south (fig. 3.13). Made of mud bricks, the fortification-wall was provided with stone veneer at strategic places, particularly at the corners. Bastions were also constructed at different points.

Fig. 3.14 Dholavira: Staircase in the northern gateway of the Castle

These were rectangular or square but not circular.

A seasonal nullah, named Mansar, flows past the northern fortification-wall, while another, called Manhar, passes along the south-east corner and then flows on the southern side of the fortified area. It is these nullahs that were bunded by the Dholavira engineers to provide regular water supply to the residents. We shall deal with these water-supply arrangements in some detail in Chapter VIII.

Within the overall enclosure walls just referred to, there lay the Middle Town and the Citadel. These also had their own fortifications. The Citadel was further divided into two parts, which have been designated by the excavator, R.S. Bisht, as Castle and Bailey (fig. 3.13). In the context of the entire

Fig. 3.15 Dholavira: Terrace in front of the northern gateway

layout it may also be noted that the various units of the settlement were not arranged in a concentric manner, i.e. the Citadel did not form the centre around which the Middle Town and then the Lower Town were located.

As might be expected, the Citadel commanded the entire scenario, with a height of 15-18 m above the surrounding ground level. Within the Citadel itself, the Castle was higher than the Bailey. A sizable portion of the Bailey has been excavated which gives an idea of the nature of the structures within it. It had residential houses, consisting of well-planned rooms, baths, drains and entrances sometimes provided with thresholds. Specially noteworthy in the Bailey was a structural complex which comprised a group of four square underground chambers, arranged in two rows of two each. More or less of the same size, each one measured approximately 3 x 3 m on plan and went to a depth of about 2.6 m. Though no cereals were recovered from the

Fig. 3.16 Dholavira: Inscription consisting of ten Harappan signs

chambers, it is likely that these were used for storage.

The nature of the structures inside the 'Castle' was quite different. It had a 13-m wide street, called the 'Broadway' by the excavator. It runs from the eastern gateway to the western, dividing the Castle into two parts, northern and southern, the latter being larger. While the eastern gate opened outside, the western connected the Castle with the Bailey. The Castle had gates on the northern and southern sides as well. We shall come a little later to the details of the northern and eastern gates which have been thoroughly excavated. Meanwhile, some more details about the structures inside the Castle.

In the area south of the Broadway, a large well has been discovered (pl. VIA). While we shall deal in Chapter VIII with details of this well including the likely mechanism used to draw water from it, here it would suffice to say that the water from it was conducted through a covered channel to feed a nearby tank measuring on plan 4.35 m north-south and 2.95 east-west (pl. VIB). It had a depth of 3.58 m. In the lower 1.4 m, the side walls were formed

Fig. 3.17 Dholavira: A view of the eastern gateway of the Castle, with pillar-bases *in situ*

by vertically placed stone slabs, while the upper part had stone-rubble masonry. Stone slabs were also used to pave the floor. Further, in the floor of this tank there was yet a smaller tank. It measured just 78 x 65 cm. At the north-eastern corner of the bigger tank there was a flight of six steps. Towards the closing days of the 1997 fieldwork traces of another tank in the neighbourhood were found. What was the purpose of these tanks? In any case, they do remind one of the Great Bath at Mohenjo-daro, which is considered to have had some religious association.

Near the commencement of the Broadway on the eastern side there stand two pillars at a distance of 3.8 m from each other. Their exact function yet remains to be determined. Equally noteworthy is the drainage system met with in the Castle. A large-sized covered drain, starting at the northern end, with cesspools and cascades, passed through the Broadway and moved on to the western gateway to enter the Bailey from where it finally discharged into the open space on the west.

The fortification-walls around the Castle were made of mud bricks to begin with but were soon provided with stone-rubble veneer. Sometimes even dressed stones were used. At one point the basal width of the wall, including the veneer, was noted to be 18.5 m. The maximum available height is 9 m.

As mentioned earlier, two gateways, one each on the northern and eastern side of the Castle have been excavated. Laid out through the northern wall, the gateway complex had an elaborate staircase (fig. 3.14). It was in the form of an 'L'. Starting from the inner side, the upper, and longer, arm of the 'L' had thirteen steps, running west-east. These led down to a landing at a depth of 2.30 m. Here the direction of the staircase changed to south-north. With another ten steps and a descent of 2 m, one landed on the floor of a passageway. At the end of this 7-m long passage there was a threshold the slabs of which had holes, evidently provided for holding a wooden door-frame. In front of this gate and running to a length of about 80 m along the fortification-wall there was an open terrace (fig. 3.15). It stretched beyond the gate to a distance of 12 m, and was 6 m in height above the ground level outside. Its likely use may have been in the context of a stadium that lay between the northern walls of the Castle and Bailey on the one hand and the southern end of the Middle Town on the other (Chapter IX).

On either side of the passage referred to above, there was a chamber, whose floors lay at a height of about 2 m above the level of the passage. The roof of these chambers rested on stone pillars, more about which will be said in the context of the eastern gateway.

One must refer here to a unique discovery from Dholavira. In one of the chambers mentioned above, there lay on the floor an inscription in the Harappan script (fig. 3.16). It conisted of ten letters, each having a height of about 35-37 cm and width of 25-27 cm depending on the nature of the letter. These letters were composed of sliced pieces of some 'crystalline material, maybe rock, mineral or paste'. While it is difficult to be sure of the exact function of this inscription (it is thought by the excavator to have been a signboard), there is little doubt that size-wise this is the largest inscription ever discovered in the Harappan domain.

The eastern gateway had all the elements that the northern one had: a staircase and a passageway with a chamber on its side. The frontal terrace was also there. However, more noteworthy were the parts of stone pillars many of which were *in situ* (fig. 3.17). Cubical, cylindrical and even *damarū*-shaped, these blocks are so well polished (pl. VIIIA) that had these not been found in the excavation, even knowledgeable scholars would have doubted their Harappan association, since no such pillars have ever been reported from any other Harappan site. Further, the only examples of polished pillars (which are no doubt much more glossy) come from the third century BC (Aśokan times) and not from the third millennium BC.

The Middle Town, located to the north of the Citadel complex and separated from it by an open space, most probably used as a stadium, had its own fortifications. The fortfication-walls as well as the streets and houses inside were all oriented along the cardinal directions. Of the gates of the fortifications, that on the east has been excavated. Its width is a little less than 3 m. The walls on either side of it measure 5.2 m in thickness. Adjacent to the two corners of the walls on each side was placed a vertical stone, evidently to function as a fender post to prevent any damage being caused to the corners. At the exterior end of the gate, slabs had been laid, some flat and some vertical and a little bit raised from the level of the flat ones. The vertical slabs have grooves in them, evidently to hold the door frame. In alignment with this gate there runs one of the major east-west streets of the Middle Town. It varies in width at places, with an average of about 5 m. Immediately to the west of fortification-wall there is a north-south street, 3.5 m in width, separating the wall from the houses in the interior. The streets inside ran on a grid pattern. While the major north-south street measured 5.75 m in width, others measured variously 2.6 m, 1.8 m and even 1.5 m, the last two being just lanes that would not permit any vehicular movement. The houses in the Middle Town were fairly large, with provision for many rooms, bathroom, etc.

The Lower Town did not have a system of fortification of its own.

However, it did lie within a fortified area, provided by the outermost fortifications of the settlement as a whole (fig. 3.13). The layout of the streets in the Lower Town was also on the grid pattern. Thus, more or less in alignment with the major east-west street of the Middle Town there was a street in the Lower Town as well. Crossing it at right angles there were two major north-south streets, besides other north-south and east-west streets and lanes.

The houses in the Lower Town also were well laid out. For example, in one of the rooms in a house dressed stones were used and what is no less interesting is that these stones followed the standard size of the Harappan bricks, viz. 40 x 20 cm x 10 cm. In another house, there were a stone-paved bathroom, stone-lined drain and a sullage pit immediately outside the house. A storage jar and a quern were found in another house. All told, the standard of the houses in the Lower Town at Dholavira does not indicate that their occupants were at a very low economic level. What then was the exact socio-economic difference between the occupants of the Middle and Lower Towns? Perhaps further detailed work may be able to answer this. As for an economically not-so-well-off class, there is an indication since there are signs of habitation even outside the fortified area.

In concluding this note on the layout and nature of the habitation at Dholavira, one does feel that further excavations ought to be carried out within the so-called 'Castle' in order to get a clear picture of the structures therein. In case it is found to contain some religious buildings, the position would be similar to that of the southern part of the 'Citadel' at Kalibangan which was found to have religious structures. In the case of Kalibangan, it may be recalled, the northern part had residential buildings and it has been surmised that in that part there lived the priests who looked after the rituals performed in the southern part. Since at Dholavira also we do have residential buildings in the 'Bailey' part of the Citadel, a lot will indeed depend on the kind of structures we finally come across in the 'Castle.' To put it in clearer terms, we have to answer: Was the Citadel at Dholarvira the seat of a secular chief or of a religious authority? Such an investigation is necessary since it would throw light on the system of governance of the Harappans. The debate is between 'king'-dom and 'priest'-dom.

CHAPTER IV

SOME OTHER SITES THAT MATTER: A PEEP INTO THE DEVOLUTION OF THE INDUS CIVILIZATION

Besides the five sites discussed in the previous chapter there are many which have been subjected to excavation and have yielded valuable results. However, we shall deal here with only some of them, highlighting their significance in the Harappan set-up.

We may begin with **Manda.** Located on the right bank of the Chenab, about 28 km north-west of Jammu, it is the **northernmost** site known so far of the Mature Harappan stage (fig. 1.2). Altogether three cultural periods have been identified, of which the upper two (Periods II and III) belong to the early historical times with which we are not concerned here. Period I is further divisible into two subperiods, viz. IA and IB. Of these, the former is comparable to the lower levels of Period II of Kalibangan, wherein Early as well as Mature Harappan pottery types co-occur. There were, of course, the other Mature artefacts like chert blades, terracotta 'cakes,' tanged arrow-heads, an unfinished seal and a few potsherds bearing graffiti. Particular mention may also be made of a double-spiral-headed copper pin.

By Subperiod IB, the Early Harappan pottery types disappeared. Instead, the excavators report the presence of 'Grey Ware elsewhere generally associated with the Painted Grey Ware'. To be noted, however, is the fact that there was no iron yet.

Ropar, now renamed Rupnagar, is the first Harappan site to have been excavated in India after Independence. Situated on the left bank of the Sutlej in Panjab, it has yielded the remains of six cultural periods, of which the lower two are associated respectively with the Mature Harappa Culture and the Painted Grey Ware Culture (Y.D. Sharma 1982). However, there was a clear break between these two periods. A cemetery was also identified at the site. The graves had the usual extended burial, but it is interesting to note that in one case a dog, perhaps a pet, was also interred along with the master.

Balu, in District Jind, Haryana, is a small Harappan site—only 200 x 80 m. Yet it was fortified during the Mature times (Period II). Period I, however, yielded the remains of the Early Harappan stage, whereas Period III showed the Harappan Culture at its decline.

This decline or devolution is reflected at many other Harappan sites in north-eastern Haryana and western Uttar Pradesh, shattering the view that the Harappan Civilization came to a sudden end one fine morning.

Mitathal, again in Haryana (District Bhiwani), is yet another site showing gradual change. Here two periods have been identified, of which Period I (earlier) has yielded Early Harappan material similar to that from Period I at Kalibangan, including bricks in the ratio of 3:2:1. Period II is divisible into two subperiods, A and B. In IIA Mature Harappan elements appeared, including the typical bricks in 4:2:1 ratio, though some pottery types of the Early stage also continued. In IIB a general decline set in and there appeared changes in the pottery shapes as well.

With the drying up of the Ghaggar-Sarasvatī system, the Mature Harappans had begun to migrate across the Yamunā. Thus, in the upper Gaṅgā-Yamunā *Doāb* we have Late Harappan sites like Hulas and Alamgirpur.

Hulas, in District Saharanpur, Uttar Pradesh, has a sizable mound, covering 330 x 170 m. However, not all of it was occupied during the Late Harappan times. In all five cultural periods were identified, of which the lowest, I, was Late Harappan. With a break, came up the second occupation characterized by the Painted Grey Ware. The succeeding periods, III-V, were associated respectively with the Northern Black Polished Ware, Śuṅga-Kushan and Gupta times. Period I has yielded a terracotta sealing with inscription in the Harappan script, as well as terracotta 'cakes' and faience beads and bangles. At the same time, the pottery showed devolutionary changes. For example, the jars had high neck with everted rim and the dishes-on-stand showed a prominently drooping rim (Dikshit 1982).

Such a change is also noticeable at **Alamgirpur** which is the **easternmost** site known so far of the Harappan Civilization. The mound, located on the left bank of the Hindon, an eastern tributary of the Yamunā, in Meerut District, Uttar Pradesh, is very small (only 60 x 50 m), but has yielded useful data. Four occupational periods were identified, of which the earliest (Period I) is Late Harappan. Periods II, III and IV belonged respectively to the Painted Grey Ware, early historical and medieval times.

In Period I there occurred the typically Mature Harappan pottery forms like perforated jars and cylindrical beakers and painted designs like intersecting circles, peacocks, etc. alongside pointed bottom goblets, dishes-on-stand with distinctively drooping rim and high-necked jars with everted rim (fig. 4.1), all of which are characteristic of the Late Harappan times in northern India. Interesting also was the discovery of a flat platter with three short legs, similar to the modern *chakalā* or *pātā* on which bread is rolled. Incidentally, it also bears a short inscription at the bottom in the Harappan script, maybe the owner's name? Cubical dice, cart-frames and terracotta 'cakes' were amongst the other typical Harappan artefacts.

Whereas at neither Hulas nor Alamgirpur was there an overlap between the Late Harappan stage and the Painted Grey Ware (PGW), an overlap was noticed at **Bhagwanpura** in District Kurukshetra, Haryana. But, it must be added, this overlap was not between the 'Late Harappan' and the PGW, but between a stage which itself was later than the Late Harappan, though it may have been derived from it in conjunction with other localized traditions. This overlap seems to have taken place in the last quarter of the second millennium BC. It may be noted that iron had not come into use so far. At the same time, interest attaches to the use of glass of which bangles in black, sea-blue and white colours were recovered.

In the southern domain of the Harappan Civilization, many a site has been excavated, but here we shall limit our discussion to only the following: Daimabad, Kuntasi, Rojdi, Bet Dwarka, Desalpur and Rangpur.

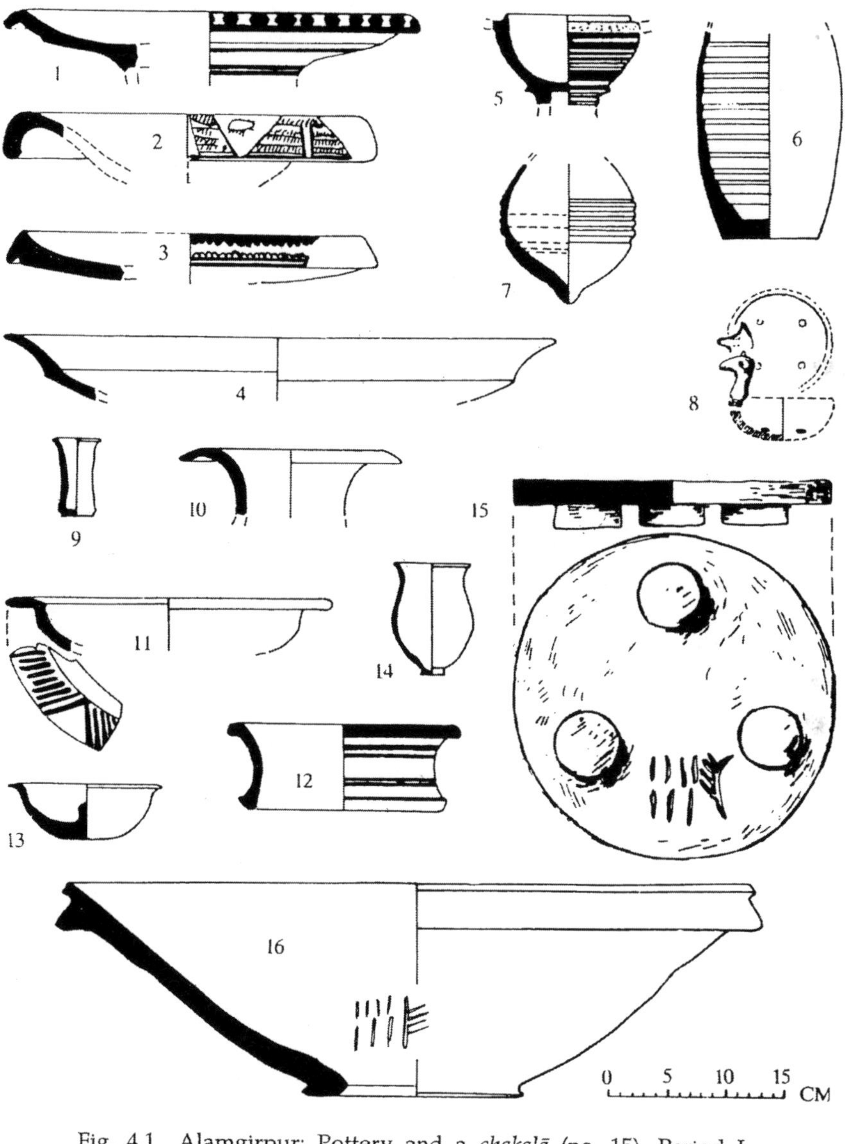

Fig. 4.1 Alamgirpur: Pottery and a *chakalā* (no. 15), Period I

Situated on the left bank of the Pravarā, a tributary of the Godāvarī, in District Ahmednagar, Maharashtra, **Daimabad** is the **southernmost** site associated with the Harappan civilization. Five cultural periods have been identified at the site, of which the Late Harappan is the second (II) from the bottom, the earliest (I) belonging to what is known as the Savalda Culture (Sali 1986). Thus the Late Harappans were not the first settlers at the site. (Periods III, IV and V are associated respectively with the Daimabad, Malwa and Jorwe Cultures.) In contrast to the Savaldans, the incoming Harappans, though late in their own tradition, did orient their houses along the cardinal directions. There also occurred button-shaped terracotta seals with the Harappan script, but these were not of the standard Harappan type. Some potsherds too bore Harappan signs which were either inscribed or painted. Interesting also was the discovery of a burial in the typical Harappan style: body laid supine in an extended position, with the head to the north. The grave was lined with bricks which had the typical Harappan ratio of 4:2:1.

However, it is on another account that Daimabad shot into prominence. In 1974, a clandestine dig at the site threw up a cache of copper objects comprising a bullock-drawn chariot (pl. VB), an elephant, a buffalo (pl. VA) and a rhinoceros, all together weighing 65 kg. The regular excavations carried out at the site have, however, given no clear evidence regarding the association of these objects with any of the cultural horizons referred to above. At the same time, it has been claimed that these may have belonged to the Late Harappan times. The chariot, intermediary pole and the bullocks together account for a length of 45 cm (pl. VB). A male figure stands on the chariot and holds a stick in the right hand, as if to make the bullocks move. In front of the figure there also stands a dog on the pole. The wheels of the chariot are solid and are in one built with the axle. Three of the features in this chariot-complex are in a way reminiscent of the Harappan tradition: (i) the solid wheels; (ii) the forward-projecting horns of the bullocks (similar to those from Chanhu-daro); and (iii) the face of the driver. But these similarities do not clinch the issue. On the other hand, the metallic composition of these figures militates against their Harappan origin. Whereas the Harappan metal objects generally have an alloy of tin with copper, there is no tin in the Daimabad specimens. If one were to think of these objects as having been the product of the Malwa or Jorwe Cultures of which settlements have been found at the site, that too does not seem to work. In the first place, these cultures are very poor in metal to have been able to produce such large-sized, heavy objects. Secondly, and this is no less important, the metal used for the Malwa/Jorwe objects has no arsenic content whereas the Daimabad objects do have the same. To this debate one might well introduce the Copper Hoard Culture which was a late contemporary of the Harappa Culture. It was essentially a culture dominating the Gaṅgā-Yamunā plains but stray Copper Hoards have been found as far down as Kallur which is way south of Daimabad. Though no such figures have so far been found along with the copper hoards, such a possibility cannot be ruled out. That, however, is purely subjective. But an objective piece of evidence that does make one think in terms of the Copper Hoard Culture is that from the metallic point of view there is a good correlation between the Daimabad objects and those belonging to the Copper Hoards. Both have arsenic and both are also without tin. In addition, in the entire gamut of Bronze Age artefacts in India it is the Copper Hoard Culture alone which can claim to have an enormous supply of copper—the well-known Gungeria copper hoard of Madhya Pradesh weighed as much as 400 kg, which is more than six times the weight of the Daimabad bronzes. However, in spite of the foregoing factors favouring a likely Copper Hoard association of the Daimabad objects, the matter has to be kept in a 'suspense account' until some more clinching stratigraphical evidence is obtained.

In Rajkot District, Gujarat, **Kuntasi** is located on the right bank of the Phalgī river which discharges into the Rann of Kachchha. A village situated opposite Kuntasi is known as Hajnali and local tradition has it that until recently Muslims used to set out from here on their *hajj* pilgrimage. It is thus not unlikely that in the Harappan days too Kuntasi may have functioned as an estuarine port.

Within a 7-m thick deposit, two cultural periods have been identified, numbered I and II from bottom upwards (Dhavalikar et al. 1996). The former yielded the Harappan black-on-red ware, including such forms as the S-shaped and ledge-necked jars. A typical Gujarati form, viz. the stud-handled bowl, was also there. In addition, there was bichrome pottery having black and brown designs on a red/buff surface. The other Harappan artefacts included cubical chert weights, carnelian beads, micro-beads of steatite and terracotta cart-frames.

Following the Harappan tradition, Kuntasi was also fortified. But the layout within was different from the usual. Streets and houses did not follow the grid pattern. Instead, the houses were laid out peripherally along the inner side of the fortifications, leaving an open space in the centre, which, for all one can guess, may have been used for community gatherings.

Ill-built houses, shrinkage of the area of occupation and a much lesser number of typical Harappan artefacts indicated degeneration in Period II. Further, the occurrence of the black-and-red ware confirmed what was happening in other parts of Kachchha, viz. the arrival of some people from the Ahar region in southern Rajasthan.

Located in the heart of the Saurashtra plateau, **Rojdi** is not a 'standard' Harappan site like Lothal in the Gujarat plains. Along with some other sites in the region, it has thrown up features which have made the excavators name this cultural assemblage as 'Sorath Harappan'. They aver (Possehl and Herman 1990: 313) that 'not more than 28 of the 98 Mohenjo-daro vessel types are found at Rojdi. Several of the most important Rojdi forms, the very common convex-sided bowl and some dish-types, seem to be absent from Mohenjo-daro.' More importantly, the subsistence pattern is different. Whereas the main Harappan cereals were wheat and barley, the Rojdians cultivated a variety of millets, such as *jowār, bājarā* and *rāgī*. This change seems to be in keeping with the local vegetation, terrain and climate.

Rojdi, situated on the bank of the Bhādar river, spreads out more along it than at right angles to it. It is thus 500 m in length, but only 150 m in width. There is evidence of a fortification-wall, about 2 m in thickness. But the houses inside are not impressive. These were made of mud on stone foundations. There was no drainage system. No seals or sealings were found, yet some members of the community seem to have been literate, as indicated by the presence of an inscribed potsherd. Some kind of trade activity is also indicated by the occurrence of a few typical Harappan weights.

Bet Dwarka, located on the north-western tip of the Kathiawar peninsula, has also yielded Harappan remains, including a seal of chank-shell with the typical three-headed-animal motif. Parts of this site have since been overtaken by the rising sea-level. It is quite likely that in ancient times, Bet (meaning 'old') Dwarka may have functioned as a port where boats plying between say Lothal in India and sites in the Persian Gulf may have halted and may have even picked up/dropped some commodities of export/import.

In this context, one must refer to another noteworthy site, **Desalpur**. Accessible through the Little Rann of Kachchha, it too may have participated in the westerly trade. Though small in size, only 130 x 100 m, the site seems to have had some importance since it was duly fortified. Amongst the Harappan objects recovered from here, special mention may be made of an inscribed seal of copper, since copper seals are rare on the Indian side of the border and are more at home at Mohenjo-daro.

While dealing with Lothal (Chapter III), we showed that by Phase B, a decline in the Mature Harappan stage had started. The fortifications had gone out of use and so also the dockyard, warehouse, etc. Town-planning and drainage were things of the past. The story of this devolution continued at **Rangpur**, a site hardly 50 km from Lothal. The earliest cultural material at this site belonged to a pre-pottery microlithic stage with which we are not concerned here. With a break in between, came up Period II of which three subdivisions, A, B and C, have been identified (Rao 1962-63). While Subperiod IIA had most of the elements of the Mature Harappan stage, such as standardized bricks, cubical weights and typical pottery, there also occurred many local pottery forms like stud-handled bowls. Decline became pronounced in Subperiod IIB wherein no kiln-fired bricks, not even mud bricks, were used. Presence of post-holes indicates that the houses were now made of wattle-and-daub. In IIC also the change continued and some new pot-forms and painted designs appeared. Period III is to be noted for its lustrous Red Ware and a black-and-red ware with white-painted designs. The change from Lothal A to Rangpur III presents a typical picture of the degeneration of the Harappan Civilization from its highly developed urban form to a rural scenario.

In concluding this chapter we may perhaps give some thought to the phenomenon of degeneration, devolution or transformation—call it by whichever name you like. It would have been noticed that both in the Ghaggar-

Sarasvatī region and in Gujarat the major difference between the antiquities of the Mature and Devolved stages of the Harappan Civilization lies in the **absence** of weights, measures, seals, sealings and use of script from the latter (besides, of course, town-planning, fortifications and monumental buildings). While dealing with the rise of the Harappan Civilization (Chapter II) we had noticed that it was the **introduction** of these very items, viz. weights, seals, script, etc. that differentiated the Mature from the Early. As already mentioned in that context, these items are clearly associable with trade. The absence or disappearance of these items would then indicate that trade had badly suffered, as a result of which these were no longer needed. This decline in and subsequent end of trade with western and central Asia is duly corroborated by the lessening and subsequent disappearance of items such as etched carnelian beads, weights, seals, etc. from those regions. With a steep fall in trade, economic levels also correspondingly went down. To this miserable situation, climatic changes, the withering out of the landscape, shifting of river-courses and a host of other factors must have contributed. All this resulted in a decline in the standard of living. In such a situation nobody would have cared for town-planning much less for the maintenace of a drainage system. Luxury items and objets d'art became things of the past. Gradually cities were abandoned and people reverted to rural areas. This shift is fully confirmed by the statistics of settlements in the late and devolved Harappan scenario. Of these times there are no cities, but only villages. To parody a part of Tennyson's famous poem, The Brook, the villages must have whispered to one another:

C'ties may come and c'ties may go
but we go on for ever.

CHAPTER V

THE EARLIEST AGRICULTURAL FIELD EVER REVEALED THROUGH AN EXCAVATION

Amongst the many noteworthy contributions made by India to our knowledge of the Indus Civilization is that of an agricultural field which dates back to the first half of the third millennium BC and is, as far as the author is aware, the earliest brought to light through an excavation. It is associated with the first occupation at Kalibangan which pre-dates the Mature Stage of the Indus Civilization (Lal 1970-71).

Before we discuss the details of this field, it may perhaps be worthwhile to share with the readers a little bit of the curiosity, suspense and subsequent excitement that we the excavators went through during the weeks that we discovered the field. In Chapter II we dealt with the layout of the Early Harappan settlement at Kalibangan. To recall, it was enclosed by a fortification-wall. In order to ascertain if there was some habitation even outside the fortified area we put up a trench about 70 m south of it. Instead of discovering any structures we came across a few dark parallel lines in the small trial pit, 1 x 1 m, that we had taken up. These ran east-west and had an intermediary distance of 30 cm. We could not make out what these lines meant and thought that these might be either furrow-marks or, more likely (as we thought at that stage), represent the decomposed remains of some fencing or similar structural device made of split bamboos. When we widened the trial pit we came across not only more of the east-west lines but also lines running at right angles to the former and themselves placed at a distance of 1.9 m from one another. To uphold our earlier speculation about these lines

Fig. 5.1 Kalibangan: Criss-cross furrows of an Early Harappan agricultural field

representing traces of a split-bamboo fencing, we thought that the lines at distances of 1.9 m might represent the cross-bars, added to strengthen the other set. However, when the trench was further widened to about 4 x 4 m and we still found both the sets of lines spreading all over the area, our bamboo-fencing theory began to recede to the background, because we argued that while a fencing can be as long as needed, it would not normally have a height of 4 m. Finally, these lines were found to cover a much bigger area, 14 x 10 m, without reaching the end (fig. 5.1), and we had to set aside the fencing theory.

We began to reconsider the furrow-theory. However, for a few days we

Fig. 5.2 Kalibangan: Modern system of ploughing, which also has the criss-cross pattern

were at our wits' end, since we were not familiar with criss-cross furrows. In search of corroborating evidence we started looking round in the neighbouring villages and, with the help of local people, were able to locate agricultural fields with this pattern of furrows. In fact, later we noted that this was the most common pattern of ploughing in the region (fig. 5.2). And now we know that this pattern is followed not only in north-eastern Rajasthan, but also in Haryana, Panjab and western parts of Uttar Pradesh. (Interestingly, this area is coterminous with the spread of the Harappa Culture in northern

Fig. 5.3 Kalibangan: Modern field with mustard plants in the widely distanced furrows and those of horse gram in the others

India, which suggests the continuity of a rural tradition.)

We may now try to explore the reasons behind the adoption of this kind of pattern by the Early Harappans (evidently also followed by the Mature Harappans). Since we cannot communicate with the Harappans to obtain their reasoning for such a pattern, we have to project the present on the past in this search. Today, the local farmers grow horse gram in the narrowly spaced east-west furrows and mustard in the widely spaced north-south ones (fig. 5.3). This, they aver, is what their forefathers have also been doing generation after generation.

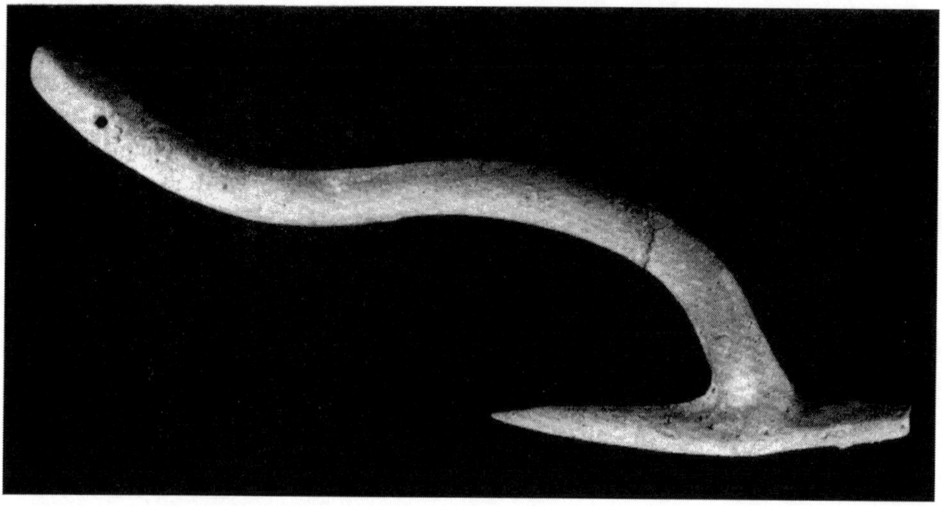

Fig. 5.4 Banawali: Terracotta model of a plough, Harappan

The aforesaid crop-patterning has to say much more than what meets the eye. Kalibangan is located on 29 degrees northern latitude, as a result of which shadows will always be cast to the north. And these shadows will be much longer in the winter season when the sun moves to the southern hemisphere. Here it also needs to be stated that both horse gram and mustard are winter crops. Also, that the mustard plants are much taller than those of horse gram. Thus, the former require a much greater space in between them than do the latter. But it is the orientation of the mustard-bearing furrows that is more significant. The mustard plants are grown in the widely distanced **north-south** furrows in order that their long shadows may not fall on the horse gram plants and prevent the latter from getting adequate sunlight. Had it been the reverse arrangement, i.e. had the mustard plants been grown in the east-west furrows (even if these were to be widely spaced), the result would have been disastrous for the growth of the horse gram plants placed in the north-south rows. Should not then full credit go to the Early Harappans to have devised a system with this kind of orientation? Once the system was found to be useful it has remained in vogue for the past five millennia.

A word about the stratigraphical horizon of this agricultural field. It was found overlain by a layer of sand, indicative of some time-gap. Above it there was a deposit bearing Mature Harappan pottery and other artefacts. This latter deposit, in turn, was associated with a Mature Harappan structure. In another part of the trench, the furrows themselves were found disturbed by clay enclosures and ash-pits carrying Mature Harappan material. It is, therefore, amply clear that this field was pre-Mature Harappan in date and may thus be placed in the first half of the third millennium BC.

While discussing the furrow-marks, it is but natural to think of the plough that may have been used in those days. As is well known, there has been a debate about the exact shape of the plough used by the Harappans. Terracotta models had no doubt been found during the excavations at Mohenjo-daro, but these were fragmentary. The Harappan levels of Banawali have yielded a complete example of a terracotta model (fig. 5.4), which gives an idea of the design of the actual plough used by the Harappans. It appears to have been made of wood, probably with a sharp metallic attachment at the end.

CHAPTER VI

ANOTHER EARLIEST: THIS TIME AN EARTHQUAKE

In Chapter II we dealt with the Early Harappan levels (Period I) at Kalibangan. To recall once again, this settlement was provided with a fortification-wall around it. Though the excavation inside was not very extensive, yet a good idea of the layout was obtained. The houses, made of mud bricks, were oriented along the cardinal directions, and the streets followed suit. There were five structural subperiods, accounting for a vertical deposit of 1.6 m.

How this Early Harappan settlement came to an end makes a fascinating story (Lal 1984). In the upper part of the accompanying photograph (fig. 6.1), one sees a black layer, ruptured at least at three places and consequently producing as many as four 'steps'. Besides, one may also observe three near-vertical cleavage lines in between the ruptured parts of this layer. Though grey and whitish layers are somewhat difficult to make out in a photograph, it may nevertheless be noted that such layers too, both above and below the above-mentioned ruptured black layer, are broken along these cleavage lines. This cleavage obviously denotes some kind of disturbance of these layers which originally must have been horizontal and without any cleavage. It is obvious that this violent shake-up took place **after** a continued occupation of the site during which these layers had been laid down and not before. It is also seen that after this violent shake-up there was no further occupation and the site was abandoned.

Evidence of such a shake-up is repeated in other parts of the site. In another photograph (fig. 6.2) may be seen two successive mud-brick walls,

Fig. 6.1 Kalibangan: Faulted strata resulting from an earthquake which brought about the end of the Early Harappan settlement

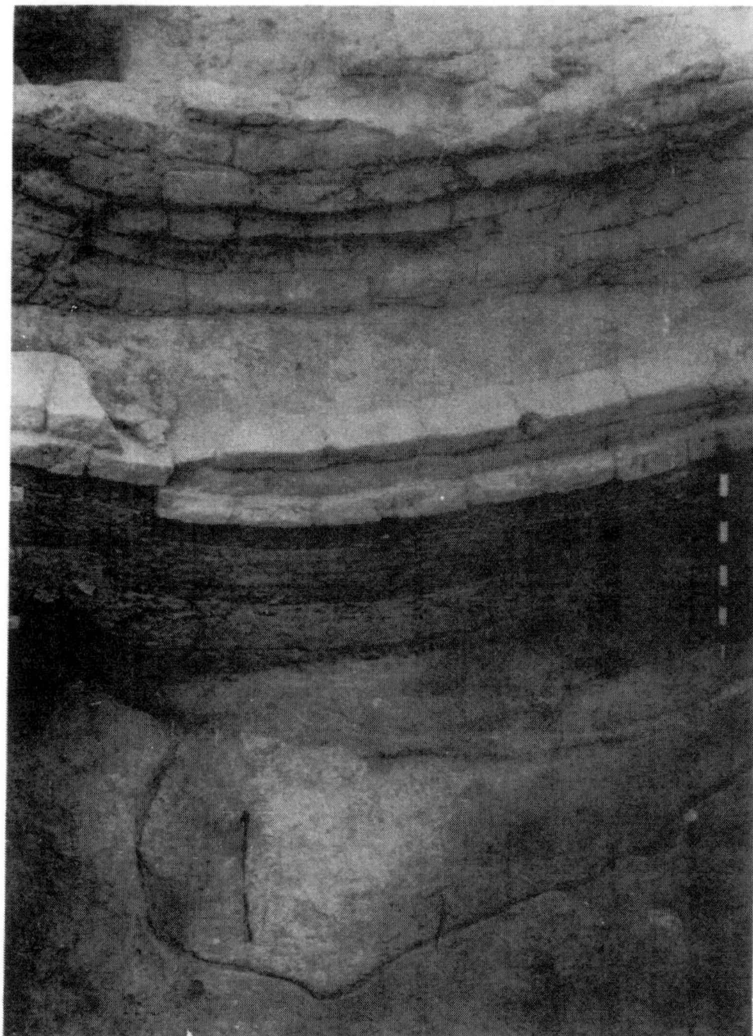

Fig. 6.2 Kalibangan: Faulted walls of the Early Harappan Period, resulting from an earthquake

sunken and cleft. The cleavage is much more pronounced in the lower wall. Further, one also notices that the successive black and grey layers immediately below the lower wall are also ruptured and follow the near-vertical cleavage-line of the wall itself.

What could have been the cause of this kind of violent disturbance which also resulted in the abandonment of the site? The most plausible explanation seems to be the occurrence of an earthquake which not only destroyed the houses but also forced the inhabitants to leave the site. This event may have taken place around 2700 BC, since, after a break, the reoccupation of the site by the Mature Harappans is ascribable, on the basis of radiocarbon dates, to ca. 26th century BC.

This then would be the earliest earthquake ever recorded in an archaeological excavation.

CHAPTER VII

THE EARLIEST DOCKYARD KNOWN TO HUMANITY

In Chapter III, while dealing with the layout of Lothal, we referred to a dockyard located immediately outside the eastern fortification-wall of the settlement (fig. 3.8). Constructed of kiln-fired bricks, the basin of the dockyard formed a rough trapezoid on plan (fig. 7.1). While its eastern and western sides measured respectively 212 m and 215 m in length, those on the north and south were much smaller, measuring only 37 m and 35 m respectively. These walls were between 1.5-1.8 m thick at the base but, tapering upwards, measured only about a metre at the top. The extant height, in the south-west corner, is 3.3 m.

Two entrances into the dockyard have been identified, one through the northern wall and the other through the eastern. That on the north was 12 m in width, while the eastern one was only 7-m wide. According to the excavator, it is the northern one that was in use first. In the southern wall there was a stepped channel through which excess water drained out.

We mentioned earlier that though today there is no river in the neighbourhood of the site, in ancient times there was one. It flowed along the western fringe of the site. This river joined the Bhogāvo which, in its turn, joined the Sābarmati, the principal river of the region. This last-named river falls into the Gulf of Khambhat which is an inlet of the Arabian Sea. Thus, a riverine link between Lothal and the sea was established.

The up-and-down plying of the boats to Lothal seems to have been as follows. Today boats from the seashore are taken to the interior via the

Fig. 7.1 Lothal: Dockyard

estuarine rivulets when high tides are on. These come back to the shore along with a receding tide. It is evidently the same practice that must have been followed in the past. In the dockyard at Lothal have also been found large stones which had been used as anchors to park the boats in position. Immediately to the west of the basin there was a wharf where the cargo was unloaded. To the west of the wharf there was a warehouse for the storage of both incoming and outgoing goods.

The warehouse was constructed of mud bricks and timber. At the base there was a large mud-brick podium, measuring 48 x 40 m on plan and 4 m in height. On it there stood a series of square mud-brick blocks, each being 3.6 x 3.6 x 0.9 m (fig. 7.2). Having an intermediary passage of 1.2 m in width, these blocks formed a grid on plan, oriented along the cardinal direction. The superstructure seems to have been that of timber (fig. 7.3), as indicated by the discovery of a charred log and plenty of ash and charcoal in the intermediary passages. When the warehouse was in operation, these passages functioned as air-ducts in order to ensure that the goods stored were not spoiled due to humidity—an annoying climatic factor in this region.

A fact to which pointed attention must be drawn is that from within these

Fig. 7.2 Lothal: A view of mud-brick blocks constituting the base of the warehouse

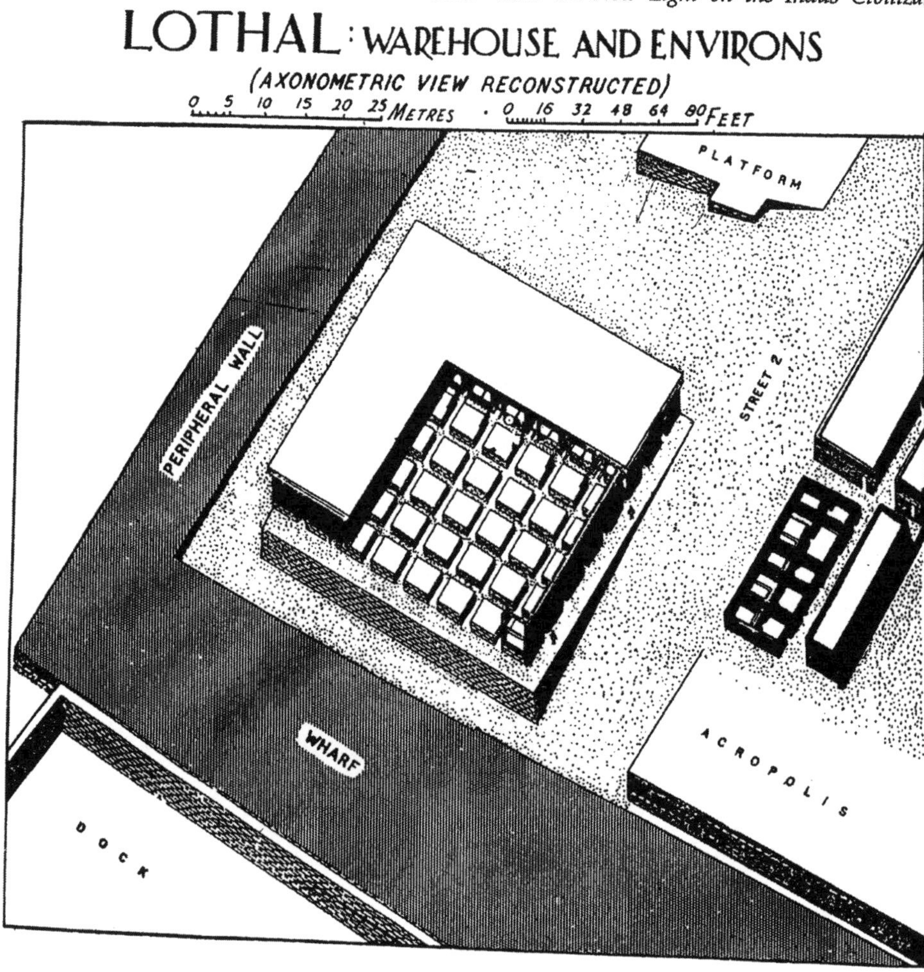

Fig. 7.3 Lothal: Warehouse and environs

passages were recovered as many as sixty-five burnt sealings of clay. These bear impressions of the wrapping fiber and knotted thread on one side and of seals with the usual animal motif and inscription on the other. This evidence leaves little doubt that in here were stored duly stamped packages which got burnt because of a fire.

Fig. 7.4 Lothal: 'Persian Gulf' seal and its impression

It often happens that when an unusual discovery is made, it brings in its trail a certain amount of controversy. And this is precisely what happened in the case of the Lothal dockyard. One of the views advanced was that it was not a dockyard but a tank for storage of drinking water. The proponents of this theory further added that the water was drawn from the tank by means of shadoofs in which the aforementioned stones were used as weights.

There are, however, quite a few factors which militate against the tank theory. In the first place, there was a river adjacent to the settlement and a number of wells within the settlement itself, which would make a potable water tank not a real necessity. Secondly, a water tank is usually provided with steps in order that people could descend to the water level, as it receded. The Lothal complex has no such steps. Thirdly, from within this complex have been found estuarine shells which would not have been the case had the tank been used for storing sweet water for drinking. In fact, the presence of estuarine shells is more in keeping with the complex having had contact with the estuaries. Finally, a more important fact that militates against the theory that the complex was used for storing drinking water is that a big drain carrying sullage from the township discharged into this basin (see fig. 3.8).

Fig. 7.5 Seal from Bahrain with Harappan inscription

In this context, we cannot but refer to the expert opinion of the then Director of Ports, Gujarat State, Shri H.P. Oza. He states: '.... It is therefore consistent to conclude on the basis of topo-sheet and our experience that a sea-passage to Lothal approachable at high tide existed.... The trapezoid brick-walled enclosure could not be meant for storing potable water. The inside face of the wall otherwise would have been sloping with steps. The alternative is that an artificial enclosure was constructed for shipping, for comfortable working of cargo and safety of boats.' (Rao 1979: 129.)

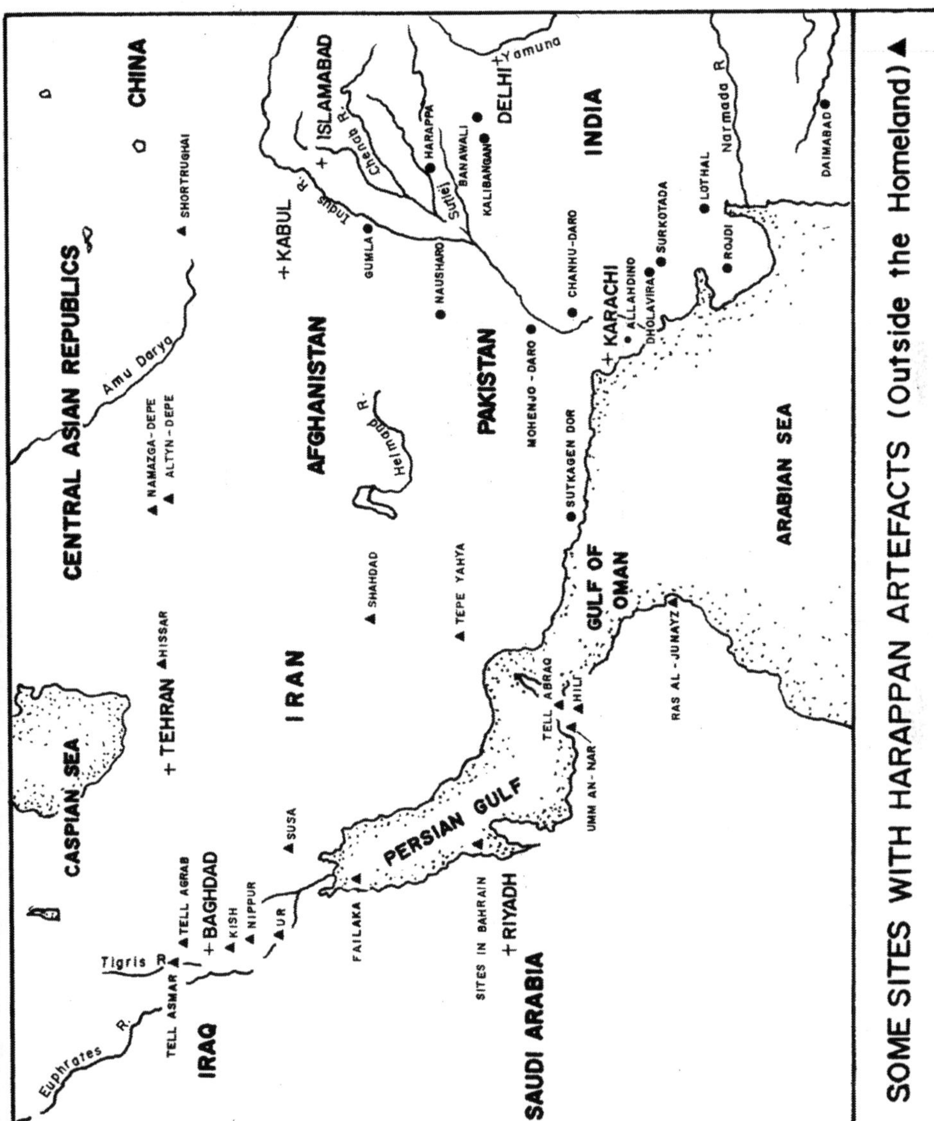

Fig. 7.6 Some sites with Harappan artefacts (outside the homeland)

Attention may also be drawn to the discovery of an unusual seal from Lothal (fig. 7.4). It is circular in shape, as against the usual Harappan ones which are square. It has a boss on one side which is perforated and bears three incised lines and four circlets. The obverse bears an engraved design which depicts (Rao 1985: 313): 'a reptile or dragon having two heads and flanked by two jumping goats or gazelle-like animals with protruding eyes and looking over the shoulder.... The goat-like animals on the seal... are more like Sumerian goats. Some of the late circular seals of Failaka... assigned by Dr. Bibby to the Sargonid period are identical in all details with the Lothal seal.' It is not unlikely that this seal belonged to a merchant from the Persian Gulf who was engaged in trade with this part of India. We have stated earlier that Lothal was an important industrial centre for the manufacture of beads of semi-precious stones, particularly the carnelian ones, which were a craze in Western Asia.

Earlier we had referred to the discovery of a variety of other objects of Harappan origin, such as square seals, chert weights, etc., in Western Asia (see here fig. 7.6). We would also like to draw attention to a seal (fig. 7.5), found recently by an Indian team during the course of excavations in Bahrain (Srivastava 1991). Though circular in shape, following the usual Persian Gulf pattern, it bears typical Harappan motifs, viz., a charging bull (or unicorn ?) and a peacock, besides an inscription in the Harappan script. It would not be unfair to speculate that, as a counterpart of the Persian Gulf merchant we just referred to, there lived in Bahrain an Indian merchant who was using this seal to conduct his business. In all likelihood the seal was manufactured, under the orders of the Indian merchant, by a local artist who perhaps having not seen a live peacock produced only a semblance of it. Anyway, Indo–Persian Gulf trade is amply attested to by these Lothal and Bahrain seals.

CHAPTER VIII

WATER MANAGEMENT: THE EARLIEST DAMS AND DRAW-WELLS

Admittedly, no settlement could ever sustain itself without adequate water supply, as is the case even now. Thus, most of the habitations had to be near some perennial source of water, such as a river or a lake. But where there was no supply throughout the year, special steps had to be taken to cope with the situation. Kalibangan had a river by its side and so was the case with Banawali, Lothal, etc. But in the case of Dholavira the source of water supply was erratic. Let us then see how the Dholavirans tackled the problem.

As mentioned earlier, two nullahs pass by the site: one, called Manhar, along the south-east corner and the other, Mansar, along the north and north-west (fig. 3.13). These, however, are not perennial but have water only when it rains. And the rains too are very erratic in this inhospitable region. It rains in short spells, but when it does rain it pours, sometimes as a cloud-burst. This erratic supply could not have been depended upon to sustain the population of such a large settlement as Dholavira. Some extraordinary devices had to be thought of and executed to cope with the situation.

Consequently, the Dholavira engineers, evidently backed by the administrative authorities, decided to harness the water that flowed through these nullahs during the short-lived rains. They dammed these nullahs and organized water supply. Although excavations have yet to be completed to obtain a detailed picture of the entire system, the available evidence indicates that the Manhar nullah was dammed at two places, one immediately to the south of the Lower Town, where even the modern engineers have put up a bund (fig, 3.13).

The other dam was built in the south-east corner where an ancient wall, running across the nullah, may still be seen on the plan (fig. 3.13). The water from this dam was taken to the open area south of the Castle where a 7-m deep and 9-m wide reservoir has been identified, the length traced so far being 79 m (pl. VIIB). It was cut deep into the bedrock, and wherever the top of the rock was at a low level a masonry wall of dressed stones was provided above it (pl. VIIA). A narrow exit channel has also been identified in the south-western corner of the tank, which carried the overflow of water further to the west. This kind of water-harnessing arrangement has not been reported from any other Harappan site in either India or Pakistan.

Equally noteworthy was the mechanism for hauling up underground water in the Castle, the upper levels of which are about 30 m above the subsoil water level today. There is not much reason to think that in antiquity the position of the subsoil water was very much different.

In Chapter III we referred to a Broadway in the Castle, which runs east-west. To the south of this Broadway has been discovered a well lined with stone masonry and having an internal diameter of 4 m. It has already been excavated to a depth of over 13 m, without reaching its bottom. Juxtaposed to a part of its circumference there is a trough made of a flat slab at the base and vertical slabs on the sides, leaving out that on the edge of the well. The trough measures 1.33 m x 1.43 m. At the bottom of the south-western corner of the trough there is a semicircular aperture in the vertical slab to let water flow out. From here the water was carried through a covered channel to a small tank the details of which have already been mentioned in Chapter III.

However, attention may here be drawn to a series of abrasion-marks on the well-side edge of the bottom (flat) slab of the trough (pl. VIA). Those who have seen such marks on similarly laid out flat slabs of troughs in the wells in rural areas of northern India would at once recognize how these marks come into being when the water is drawn. However, since not many readers may be familiar with this system it is being spelt out in some detail. (In fact, with the installation of electrically operated pumps even in rural areas this system is fast becoming obsolete.)

In the system just referred to, water from the well is drawn by means of a large-sized leather bag. It is made from the skin of an animal (usually a buffalo), the body serving as a container and neck as a nozzle to pour the water out (see pl. VIB). In the upper part of the body, a wide opening is made through which water is filled in when the entire contraption is dipped into the water of the well. To this opening as well as to the nozzle, ropes are tied in order to pull the whole thing up. In tying the respective ropes, however, it is ensured that the nozzle part remains higher so that the water is not drained out when the bag is being lifted. Of these two ropes, the one tied to the mouth or opening passes over a pulley which is supported by a framework placed above the brim of the well. The frame consists of three rods, two of which are placed vertically and the third, placed horizontally, is attached to the upper ends of the former two. It is this horizontal rod that passes through the pulley and enables it to rotate. The other rope, tied to the nozzle of the bag, passes **against** the edge of the flat slab of the trough. And it is because of the constant rub of the rope against the slab that marks are created. In this context one is tempted to recall a Hindi saying, viz. *Karata karata abhyāsa ke jaḍamata hota sujāna; rasarī āwata jāta te sila para parata nisāna*. Freely translated, it means that even a dullard can acquire the necessary intelligence only if he keeps on assiduously doing his job, just as even a rope, which is much weaker in strength than a stone slab, ultimately leaves abrasion-marks on the latter.

To revert to the method of drawing water from deep wells in the rural areas. Since the water has to be drawn from a very great depth, human labour is inadequate. Hence bullocks are used. The above-mentioned two ropes are tied to the yoke that is placed over the necks of the bullocks. In order that the bullocks may not be put to a very great strain, their pathway is specially made in a slope. Thus, while pulling up the filled leather bag the bullocks move down the slope which makes their job relatively easier and when the empty bag goes down into the well, they have little strain in moving upwards.

CHAPTER IX

THE ONLY STADIUM THAT THE HARAPPANS CAN BOAST OF

At no site of the Harappan civilization in Pakistan—even at the big ones like Mohenjo-daro and Harappa—nor even at any sites in India has a stadium been discovered. The exclusive privilege in this regard goes to Dholavira. Here the excavator, R.S. Bisht, has identified the open area between the Castle and Bailey on the one hand and the Middle Town on the other as a stadium (fig. 3.13).

Both the Castle and the Bailey have a gate through their northern fortification-walls. These provided access to the stadium. On both sides of these gates, juxtaposed to the fortification-walls, there are narrow terraces descending down to the level of the stadium. Similar terraces have also been noted on the opposite side, i.e. on the southern face of the Middle Town. It is thought that the spectators were seated on these terraces to watch what was going on in the stadium. Of what went on, however, there is little evidence to assess. The floor of the stadium was plastered over with a mixture of sand and clay and, incidentally, a human footprint impressed on this plaster has also been recovered.

The inhabitants of the Lower Town could have entry into the stadium through a gate in its eastern enclosure wall. Measuring 3.6 m in width, this gate could permit entry of bullock-carts, in case we envision a bullock-cart race. Since a stadium is an altogether new concept to be associated with the Harappan cultural milieu, it is not unlikely that this discovery may give rise to a debate, which, of course, is always welcome. The late 1960s and early 1970s witnessed a similar debate on the Lothal dockyard, which has since subsided in its favour.

CHAPTER X

FROM LEFT TO RIGHT OR RIGHT TO LEFT ? CLINCHING EVIDENCE THAT PUT AN END TO THE CONTROVERSY OVER THE DIRECTION OF WRITING IN THE HARAPPAN SCRIPT

Ever since the discovery of the Harappan script in the early 1920s, attempts have been made by many scholars, Indian as well as foreign, to decipher it. While some read a Dravidian language in the inscriptions, others, the Sanskrit. In fact, one German scholar reads even Vedic verses in the inscriptions on the seals. An interesting point about these decipherments, however, is that even in their own groups, no two Dravidianists, and likewise no two Sanskritists, agree about their readings. The present writer has reviewed many of these attempts from time to time and shown that nobody has really hit the mark. Most of them have faulted in their methodology and thus the results are bound to be wrong (Lal 1970, 1974 and 1983).

Let alone decipherment, for quite some time there was controversy over even the direction of writing in the Harappan script. Some read it from left to right, while others did it the other way round. Kalibangan has produced a few potsherds the inscribed letters on which overlap, throwing valuable light on the direction of writing (Lal 1966).

In this context, it may perhaps be of interest to the reader to know how the idea that an overlap of letters might resolve the problem regarding the

Fig. 10.1 Kalibangan: Inscribed potsherd. The overlap of letters shows that the direction of writing in the Harappan script was from right to left

Fig. 10.2 Kalibangan: Another inscribed potsherd with a similar feature

direction of writing struck the author. On a rainy day he was taking his car out of the garage. He first took it back to the left and then forward to the right in which direction the exit was located. Meanwhile, someone came in to meet him. The author stepped out of the car and began talking to the visitor. After the visitor had left and the author was about to open the door to re-enter the car, his eyes fell on the tyre-marks which were rather deep since the ground had turned muddy due to the rains. He observed that the earlier marks, made when the car was taken backward to the left, were overridden by the later ones, made when the car was driven forward to the right. He further noted that at the point of intersection, the edges of the earlier tyre-marks were obliterated by those of the later tyre-marks whereas the edges of the later tyre-marks remained intact. A kind of wishful thinking ran across the mind of the author, namely if he were to get in his excavations which were going on at Kalibangan a few inscribed potsherds with overlap of letters, it may perhaps be possible to determine which letters were written first and which afterwards. Strangely, the wishes were fulfilled and we did find a few potsherds with overlap of letters. Here we shall deal with two of them.

On one of the potsherds (fig. 10.1) may be seen three signs. If there were more on the right the same cannot be determined since the potsherd is broken at this end. However, judging from the interspacing between the signs and the blank space to the left of the 'V'-shaped sign on the extreme left, it is evident that there was no further sign on this side. The question then is: Was this 'V'-shaped sign the first or the last, that is whether the inscription began with this sign or ended with it.

The sign on the extreme right (as available now) is what is generally known as the 'fish' symbol. Its main body is formed of two opposing arcs, placed in such a way that their upper ends meet at a point, while the lower parts intersect each other. It would be seen that at the point of intersection the right-hand arc overrides the other. This would mean that the former was inscribed after the latter. The 'fish' sign usually has an oblique stroke on each side, emerging from its middle level. While the right-hand stroke is no longer there because of the breakage of the potsherd at this point, one can see the left-hand one. Its upper end slightly overlaps the left-hand arc and it is seen that at the point of overlap the upper end of the oblique stroke overrides the arc, though it does not cross over to the other side.

The middle sign consists of three parts: one resembling the English letter 'I' in its script form; another having four oblique strokes; and a third one resembling an 'angle' with the apex up. It would be seen that the group of four strokes overrides the 'I'-like part. Of these strokes, the one on the extreme right also overrides the tail-end of the oblique stroke on its right which constitutes a part of the 'fish' symbol. Further, the right-hand arm of the 'angle' overrides the lower end of the 'I'. It is thus clear that the 'I'-like part was inscribed first and then came the 'angle.'

Proceeding to the 'V'-like sign on the extreme left one sees that its right-hand arm overrides the lower end of the left arm of the 'angle' on its right.

Further, from the upper end of the 'V' sign there emerge two oblique strokes on the right and two on the left. While the two right-hand strokes are of the normal size, of the two left-hand strokes the lower one is unusually long. It represents a kind of 'flourish' which is generally seen at the end, as, for example, at the tail-end of one's signatures.

From the above discussion it is clear that the 'fish'-like sign on the extreme right was inscribed first. Then came the midlle sign with its 'I'-like and 'angle' components; and finally the 'V'-like sign on the extreme left.

The other potsherd discussed here is also broken (fig. 10.2). The result is that the sign on the extreme right is not clear; perhaps it was the 'fish' sign. The sign in the middle consists of four vertical strokes in the upper part, two in the lower, and a horizontal stroke in between. It is the delineation of this horizontal line that is important in the present context. Normally this horizontal line is of a limited length—such as seen on the right side. However, through the inadvertence of the scribe, it has gone a long way to the left. The result is that the right-hand vertical stroke of the 'V'-like sign on the left overrides the horizontal line of the middle sign. This clearly shows that the middle sign was inscribed first and then came the 'V'-like sign on the left.

Both the foregoing examples clearly demonstrate that the direction of writing in the Harappan script was from right to left.

To test-check if the conclusion arrived at through overlap-determination was really sound, recourse was taken to another methodology. In his excavation at Harappa, Vats had discovered a seal which has an inscription running along three of its edges. Fig. 10.3 presents its impression which is the positive. For a comparative study of this inscription, two persons were asked each to write out a sentence along the edges of a square piece of paper. One did it in the Arabic script which is written from right to left (fig. 10.4). The other wrote it in the Roman script the direction of which is from left to right (fig. 10.5).

It would be observed that in both cases the first line runs from one corner to the other. The second line in the Arabic example (fig. 10.4) runs along the

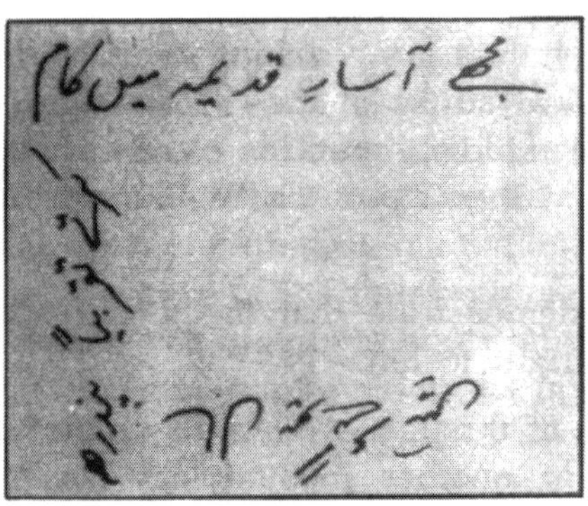

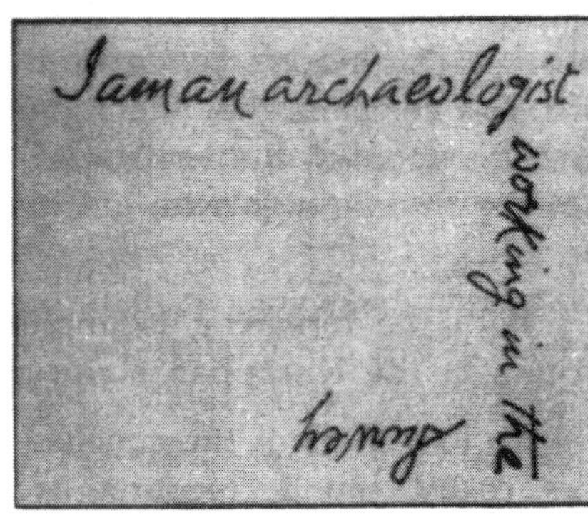

Fig. 10.3 (top) Harappa: Impression of a seal, showing an inscription running along its three edges

Fig. 10.4 (bottom left) An inscription in Arabic script which is written from right to left. It may be observed that the Harappan example (fig. 10.3) follows the Arabic pattern

Fig. 10.5 (bottom right) An inscription in Roman script which is written from left to right. The behaviour in this case is just the opposite of what happens in the Harappan example (fig. 10.3)

left-hand edge. Further, since there were already some letters of the first line in the left-hand upper corner, the second line starts from below these letters. It, however, continues right up to the bottom corner on the left. The third line does not start at the bottom-left corner because some letters were already there, but continues freely to a point where the sentence runs out. Had the sentence been longer, the letters of the third line would have continued up to the right-hand bottom corner. Finally, if some words of the sentence were still left, these would have been accommodated in the space available leaving out the upper and lower corners along the right-hand edge, since these were already occupied.

In the case of the Roman-script example (fig. 10.5), the second line runs along the right-hand edge. Further, it does not commence at the right-hand upper corner since a few letters of the first line were already there. The second line, however, continues right up to the right-hand lower corner. The third line does not start at the right-hand lower corner since it was already full. It, however, continues to a point where the sentence finishes. If there was more matter, the third line would have continued right up to the left-hand lower corner. And if some part was still left that would have gone along the left-hand edge, leaving out, of course, the lower and upper corners which were already occupied.

Let us now compare these two examples with the impression of the Harappan seal (fig. 10.3). It would at once be seen that Harappan impression follows the pattern of the Arabic inscription and **not** that of the Roman one. Thus, it gets established that the direction of writing in the Harappan seal was from right to left.

Way back, when these results were presented at an international conference in New Delhi, some scholars, known for their view that the Harappan inscriptions must be read from left to right, came up with a strange argument. They said that the direction of writing need not necessarily be the direction of reading. Luckily, a little later the author came across some potsherds in the collection of what was then called the Central Antiquities Collection. These had been found by Aurel Stein at Tor-Dherai in northern Baluchistan. They bear inscriptions in black paint, some in the Brāhmī script

Fig. 10.6 A potsherd bearing a painted inscription in Kharoṣṭhī script from Tor-Dherai. This script is known to have been written from right to left which is also confirmed by the overlap between some of the painted letters

and others in Kharoṣṭhī. It is well known that while the Brāhmī was written and read from left to right, the Kharoṣṭhī was written and read the other way round, i.e. from right to left.

The painted potsherd illustrated here (fig. 10.6), bears several letters in the Kharoṣṭhī script. Of these, the first four from the right show partial overlaps. A closer examination would show that the lower left adjunct of the first letter on the extreme right is overridden by the lower part of that on the left. Similarly, the top horizontal stroke of the second letter is overridden by the vertical stroke of the third letter. Again, the horizontal stroke of the third letter is overridden by the long oblique stroke shooting up from the next letter on the left. Such an overlap proves, in its own way, that the direction of writing in this (Kharoṣṭhī) script was from right to left, which is also known to be the established direction of its reading. Thus, the argument that the direction of writing ought not to be taken as the direction of reading is untenable and cannot offset the conclusion arrived at from the evidence of the above-discussed two potsherds from Kalibangan.

However, before we close this chapter on the direction of writing (and reading) in the Harappan script it needs to be mentioned that whenever a given inscription ran into a second line, the direction was boustrophedon, i.e. the second line, being a continuation from the last letter of the first line, started from the left. There is a very small number of inscriptions in which the direction of writing is from left to right. One does not know why it was so. Whatever the reason, these cases are but examples of the famous saying, 'exceptions only prove the rule'.

CHAPTER XI

DO SOME FOLK TALES GO BACK TO THE HARAPPAN TIMES?

Like other Harappan sites, Lothal too has yielded a rich harvest of Harappan painted pottery, but with a difference. A few of the paintings from this site set one wondering if some of the folk stories prevalent in the country had their ancestry as far back as the Harappan times. Here we shall take up two such examples.

A painting on a small vase depicts a deer and a crow, the main actors of the story, along with a pitcher in between them (fig. 11.1). There are two trees, one in front of the deer and the other between the deer on the one hand and the pitcher and crow on the other. The portrayal of the front legs of the deer indicates that it is in the process of moving away. However, with its head turned backwards, it is looking, as if in amazement, at the crow. The crow's beak is just above the pitcher, as if it has just taken it out of the latter. This scene reminds one of the story of 'The Thirsty Crow'. According to this story, the deer, though keen to drink water from the pitcher, could not do so since the water-level in it was low and it could not insert its neck to that depth. Disappointed, just when it started walking away, the wise crow collected some tiny pebbles, dropped them in the pitcher so as to raise the water-level and quenched its thirst.

The other painting seems to portray the story of 'The Cunning Fox'. A large S-shaped jar, so very diagnostic amongst the Harappan pottery-types, is profusely painted (fig. 11.2). By and large there are geometric motifs. But on a part of it there is a narrative. On the branches of a large tree two birds

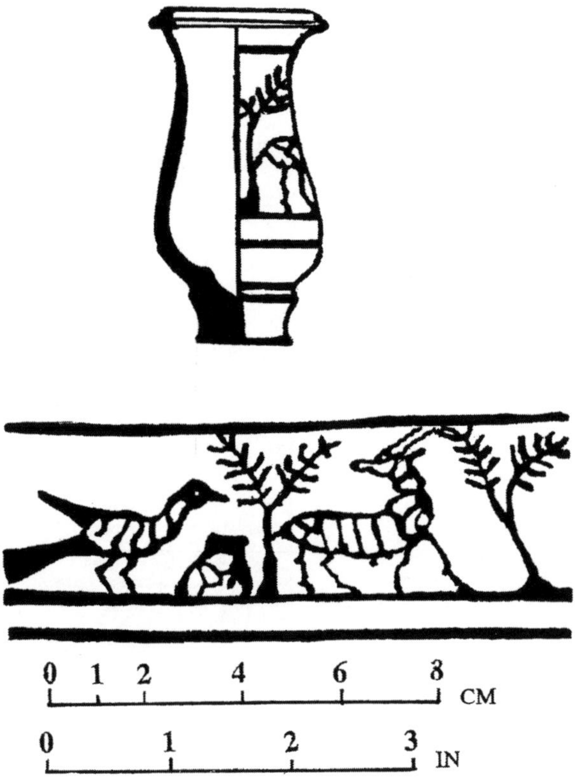

FIG. 11.1 Lothal: A vase, the painting on which probably depicts the folk tale, 'The Thirsty Crow'

are perched. Each holds a fish in its beak. The bodies of the birds as well as of the fish are cross-hatched. It may also be noted that the artist has a sense of perspective: the front bird and fish are relatively bigger than the ones behind. Above these two birds may be seen the legs of other birds, indicating that they have just flown away. The lower right-hand part of the panel is damaged. But one may still note some object hatched in a manner similar to that of the birds and the fish. In the lower left-hand part of the panel there is a solidly-filled animal whose legs and tail can be made out. Close by is a hatched object. Though one cannot be too sure of the identification of the animal, it is not unlikely that it may have been a fox, as suggested by its tail. If that be so, the story intended to be depicted may have been, as stated earlier, that of the cunning fox. As the story goes, there was a fox which wanted to take away the morsel of food which the bird was holding in its mouth. The fox got an idea, namely that it should praise the bird saying that the latter was a good singer and request it to give a demonstration of the same. The simple-minded bird did not realise the motive of the fox and succumbed to

Fig. 11.2 Lothal: A painted jar. One of the panels probably depicts the folk tale, 'The Cunning Fox'

its persuations. According to the story, as soon as the bird opened its mouth, the morsel fell down and the cunning fox made away with it. In the present depiction the bird is shown holding the fish in its beak. Obviously, the other part of the story, viz. that the bird dropped the morsel could not simultaneously be depicted. But the depiction of an object hatched in the style of the fish, close to the fox, is suggestive of the piece that fell from the bird's mouth and was taken away by the fox.

As already mentioned, the identification of these narratives is most likely to be correct, but cannot be proved. Proof could have come only if there were titles underneath. And even if there were such titles, who could have decoded the same, since the Indus script, alas!, still remains undeciphered?

CHAPTER XII

NEW LIGHT ON RELIGION: 'FIRE-ALTARS' AND ANIMAL SACRIFICE

As is well known, there are two aspects of religion: one, metaphysical or philosophical and the other ritualistic. Usually, the former is dealt with in the texts while the latter can be made out from the material remains. In the case of the Harappan Civilization we do not have any such texts. Further, whatever information could have been gleaned from the seals which seem to depict some religious motifs/scenes, the same is withheld from us since no one has really been able to decipher the Harappan script. Incidentally, it may be of interest to know that a German scholar (Richter-Ushanas 1992) has even gone to the extent of reading verses from the *Ṛigveda* in the inscriptions on some of the seals.

A seal from Mohenjo-daro depicts a figure seated on a dais and surrounded by animals like buffalo, rhinoceros, elephant, etc. It seems to have three faces, though the depiction is not very clear. Most scholars have taken the figure to represent Śiva in the form of *Paśupatī* (Lord of Beasts). That a form of Śaivism may have been one of the religions practised by the Harappans is also suggested by the occurrence of some objects made of limestone, alabaster, etc. which have been taken to represent the *liṅga*. Likewise, a few objects have been taken to be *yonis*. Some of the terracotta figurines have been taken to represent the Mother Goddess.

However, the Indian excavations have brought to light two altogether new aspects of the Harappan religion. These are: (i) a kind of worship associated with fire; and (ii) animal-sacrifice.

Fig. 12.1 Kalibangan: A 'fire-altar' in a house in the Lower Town

In an earlier chapter we referred to the layout of Kalibangan. To recall briefly, the settlement was divided into two parts, named the Lower Town and the Citadel. While the Lower Town was the general habitational area, the Citadel had an exclusive pattern. It was divided into two parts, the northern having residential houses, but the southern studded with many raised platforms with special structural features thereon.

In many houses in the Lower Town, a room seems to have been reserved for what have been called 'fire-altars' in the absence of a better term. (It must, however, be clarified that these altars have nothing to do with the fire-altars

Fig. 12.2 Kalibangan: A row of seven 'fire-altars' in the southern half of the Citadel

of the Parsis.) Roughly rectangular, with the ends somewhat rounded, these altars measured, on an average, about a metre in length and 50 cm in width (fig. 12.1). However, unlike the Parsi altars, these were sunk into the ground, to a depth of about 25 cm. The sides were plastered with mud. Within it there stood a central stele of clay, sometimes fired, measuring about 30-40 cm in height. It was usually cylindrical with a diameter of about 10-15 cm, but sometimes it could be faceted. Around it there lay circular-biconvex 'cakes' of clay, as if placed as offerings. The presence of ash and charcoal fully attested to the association of these altars with fire. Another interesting feature

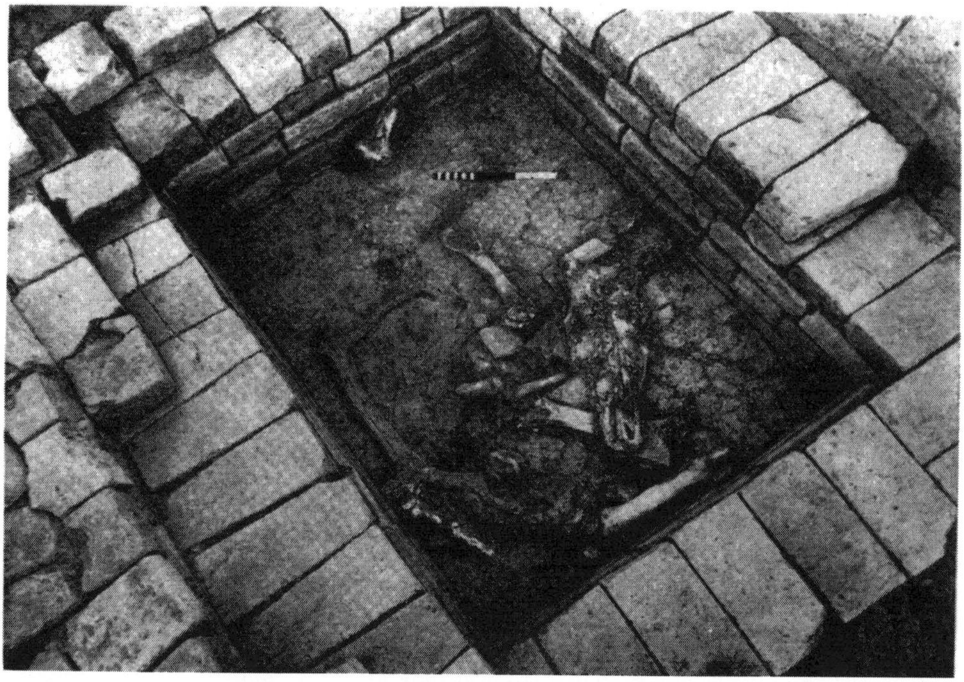

Fig. 12.3 Kalibangan: Brick-lined sacrificial pit with bones, in the southern half of the Citadel

was that these altars were located in such a way that anybody offering worship would have to face the east.

In the Citadel, on one of the platforms in the southern part there were seven contiguous altars. Though somewhat disturbed over the years, these too had the basic elements, viz. central stele, 'cakes', ash and charcoal (fig. 12.2). Embedded into the ground close by there was a pot which also contained ash and charcoal. It would indicate that fire was kept ready in the pot to be used at the time of worship. Immediately to the east of this row of altars there was a north-south wall, which made it obligatory for anyone using the altars to face the east.

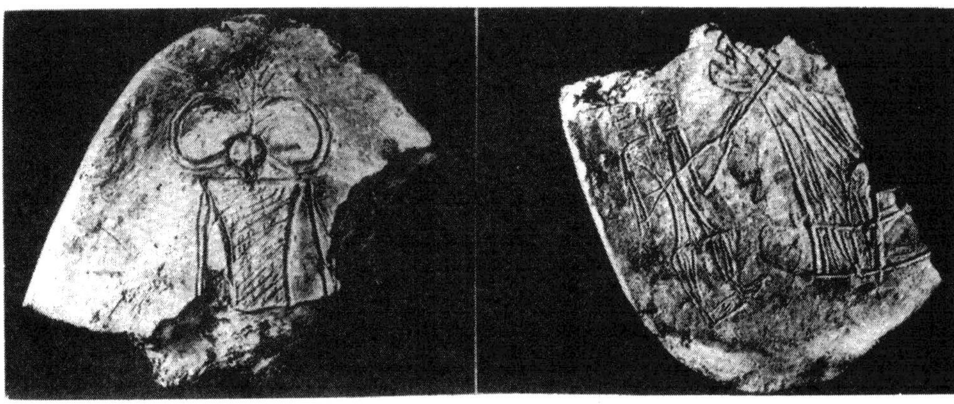

Fig. 12.4 Kalibangan: Terracotta 'cake', depicting on one side a horned deity and on the other an animal pulled with a rope by a man

A further noteworthy point about these fire-altars in the Citadel was their association with a well, bathing pavement and a drain, all of which were located hardly a few metres away. This kind of disposition would suggest that anyone offering worship at these altars was required to take a ritual bath.

To the east of the Lower Town there was a small mound (KLB-3; fig. 3.1) which yielded nothing but the remains of fire-altars, within an enclosure wall. It would appear that whereas the fire-altars in the individual houses in the Lower Town were meant for the private use of the occupants concerned, the fire-altars in the Citadel and those in the enclosure to the east of the Lower Town were perhaps meant for a kind of community worship.

On another platform in the southern part of the Citadel there was a pit, measuring 1.5 m x 1 m on plan and lined with kiln-fired bricks. In it were found bovine bones and antlers, suggesting animal sacrifice (fig. 12.3). That

Fig. 12.5 Kalibangan: Partition-wall of the Citadel with its tower, and brick-on-edge pathway

this may have been really the case is endorsed by what one sees engraved on a terracotta cake from Kalibangan itself (fig. 12.4). On one side is depicted an animal with a noose around its neck, the rope being handled by a person in front of it, in an attempt to draw it forward. On the other side of the cake there is a figure wearing a horned and feathered headgear. On the basis that the headgear is similar to that worn by the famous Śiva figure on the seal from Mohenjo-daro (mentioned earlier), it is most likely that the engraved figure under discussion may also be a deity, to whom the animal was to be offered as a sacrifice.

As stated earlier, the Citadel was divided into two parts, a northern and a southern by a medial partition wall. While the aforementioned fire-altars and sacrificial pit stood on platforms in the southern part, in the northern part, close to the medial wall and parallel to it there ran a wide, east-west pathway paved with mud bricks (fig. 12.5). It led to a point where there was a stepped passage through the medial wall interconnecting the two parts. In the northern part there were houses in which might have dwelt the priests who looked after the rituals in the southern part. In this entire context, it is tempting to surmise that on specified occasions the priests residing in the northern part assembled at the start of this specially laid out pathway and marched in a procession towards the entrance in the medial wall and moved on to the platform concerned for performing and/or supervising the ritual. This idea of a procession emanates from a ritualistic scene on a seal from Mohenjo-daro where as many as seven human figures have been shown following one another, as if in a procession.

Kalibangan does not stand alone in providing evidence of fire-altars and animal-sacrifice. Banawali and Lothal also join hands in corroboration. For example, in the habitation area at Banawali there was not only a fire altar but the area around it was found enclosed by a wall which formed an apse at one end. The complex is thought to have been an apsidal 'temple'. Whether a temple or not, it is amply clear that the fire-altar ritual, whatever its exact details, was practised by the Banawalians as well. Far south, in Gujarat, the position was no different. Lothal, too, has yielded ample evidence of fire-altars. Besides being rectangular in shape as at Kalibangan, the Lothal examples were circular as well (Rao 1979: 216-18). In respect of another site excavated by Rao in Gujarat, viz. Rangpur, he (1962-63: 47) refers to 'some indications of a ritual involving domestic fire-worship throughout the occupation.'

Animal-sacrifice is also attested to by the evidence from Lothal. Over here, in a house ascribable to Phase III (Mature Harappan) was encountered a mud platform with a mud-brick enclosure on it, the latter measuring 85 cm x 75 cm on plan and about 20 cm in depth. Within this enclosure there lay charred fragments of bovine bones, a carnelian bead and a disk-shaped pendant of gold, besides plenty of ash and charcoal. The excavator, therefore, avers that 'the platform must have been used as a sacrificial altar and the mud-brick enclosure as a sacrificial pit.'

From the foregoing evidence it would be seen that the Harappans of the Sarasvatī valley and Gujarat region were practising some kind of fire ritual and animal-sacrifice, besides, of course, sharing the other religious beliefs of the Harappans in the Indus valley.

CHAPTER XIII

WAS THE HARAPPAN SOCIETY STRATIFIED? AN ANALYSIS BASED ON NEW EVIDENCE

One would naturally like to know if there was any stratification in the Harappan society. Were all the inhabitants socially at the same level, or at different? And if they stood at different levels, what was the basis of this differentiation? Religious, economic or a combination of the two, or even of other factors? Hardly any serious attempt has been made to answer the question. Now that we have a good deal of data from so many Indian sites, we may as well look into the problem and see if we can make some sense out of these.

In Chapter III we dealt with the layout of Kalibangan, Banawali, Lothal, etc. Here we shall analyse if these data throw any light on social hierarchy.

To begin with Kalibangan. We saw that the settlement was divided into two major segments, called the Lower Town and the Citadel. We also noted that the Lower Town contained fairly large residential houses, often with a well and provision for keeping cattle in the courtyard. The entrances were wide enough to permit entry of bullock-carts which were evidently parked in the courtyard. In some houses the floors of the rooms were paved with mud bricks and even with decorated tiles. Storage jars, piled one over another, were noticed in certain cases. From many houses seals, sealings and weights were also recovered. All told, the picture seems to be that the Lower Town, with its well laid out houses, wide streets, rich yield of antiquities and a protective peripheral wall around, was occupied by those who were fairly well-to-do, engaged in agriculture and trade. They seem to have provided the economic backbone to the entire settlement.

In marked contrast, the Citadel had an altogether different kind of layout. Smaller than the Lower Town in size, it was further divided into two parts, northern and southern, by a medial wall. In the northern part only one street was noted, on either side of which there were juxtaposed houses. None of these was extraordinarily big so as to be called a 'palace'. In the southern half there were a series of mud-brick platforms over which there stood structures of a religious character, such as public 'fire-altars' and sacrificial pits. It appears that in the northern part there lived the priests who supervised the religious activities in the southern half. Altogether, therefore, there is also evidence of a priestly class in the Harappan society.

The area to the south of the Citadel was not fully excavated. But even from the limited excavation it became clear that houses over here were relatively small and that the area was **not** fortified. In a part of it a lot of pottery-waste was also observed, suggesting that here lived some potter-family. The overall picture seems to be that this unfortified area was occupied by the workers' class who, besides carrying out such jobs as pottery-making, may have attended to the needs of the residents of the Lower Town and the Citadel.

Such a dispensation would seem to suggest at least a threefold division of the Harappan society, viz. a priestly class occupying the northern part of the Citadel, an agricultural-cum-mercantile community residing in the Lower Town and a workers' class located outside the two fortified areas. This kind of evidence is also available from sites like Banawali and Lothal. It would thus appear that the Harappans did have a kind of hierarchical social order.

Archaeological data often tempt one to speculate. And here is one such speculation. Did the above-mentioned three classes in the Harappan society ultimately give rise to the later-day castes: the priestly class to the Brāhmanas, the mercantile-cum-agricultural community to the Vaiśyas, and the workers' class to what came to be the Śūdras? During the Harappan times there is not much evidence of warlike activities. Thus, a Kṣatriya class may not have existed then, but may have come into being as and when the need arose.

CHAPTER XIV

DISPOSAL OF THE DEAD: SOME ALTOGETHER NEW ASPECTS. CREMATION? SYMBOLIC BURIAL? BEGINNING OF MEGALITHISM? ORIGIN OF THE *STŪPA*?

Way back when Mackay did not come across any burials during the course of his excavations at Mohenjo-daro, he averred that cremation may have been the chief mode of the disposal of the dead. However, hardly had the ink of Mackay's report dried that K.N. Shastri brought to light regular burials of the Harappans at the type-site itself. The site was subjected to further detailed excavation by Wheeler who exposed a number of burials located in a cemetery called R-37. The method of the disposal was briefly as follows. In a rectangular pit, the dead body was laid supine and fully extended. The head was invariably on the north. Along with the body were placed pottery and some food-items, probably under the belief that these might be of use to the dead in his/her journey to the next world. Sometimes the dead continued to wear their jewellery. Also placed alongside were objects of toiletry, such as mirrors, antimony rods, etc. In one case the body was found encased in a wooden coffin; in another the grave was lined with mud bricks; and in yet another case there was a mud-brick tumulus over the grave, signifying that here lay someone in particular.

The excavations at Kalibangan have not only replicated the type of burial found at Harappa but have also brought to light evidence which is new and at the same time intriguing. A normal Harappa-type burial is shown in fig. 14.1. Here the rectangular grave-pit was lined with mud bricks which were

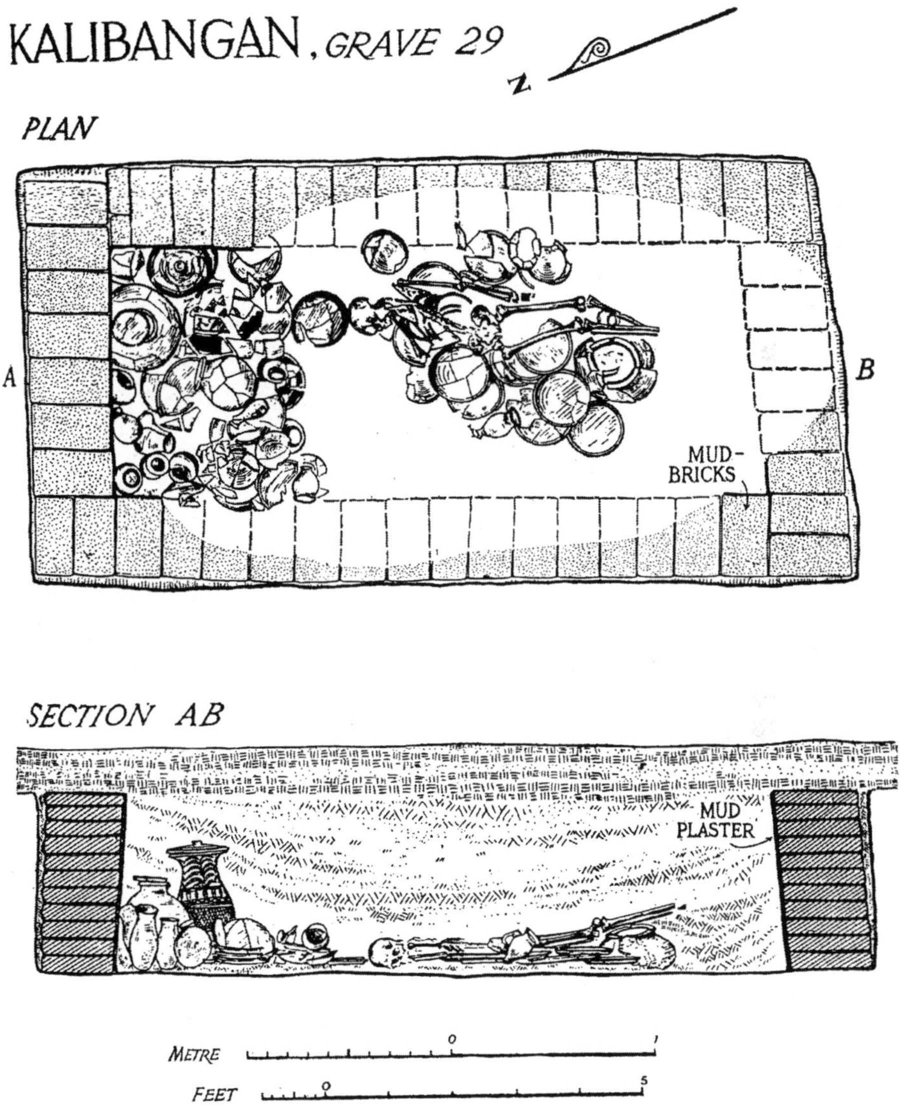

Fig. 14.1 Kalibangan: Grave 29

Fig. 14.2 Lothal: Grave with two skeletons

given a coating of mud plaster. The body lay supine in an extended position, with the head on the north. The pottery assemblage was very rich: while thirty-five pots lay below the body, as many as thirty-seven had been placed on the northern side of the head.

Within the same cemetery area, however, there were graves which had pots and even beads, bangles, etc. but no body, complete or even fractional. Further, it was noted that these graves contained successive layers of sand and clay. The absence of human body and the presence of sand-and-clay deposits need a satisfactory explanation. If one is allowed to hazard guesses, one possibility may be that, to begin with, the body was placed in these graves and after the performance of some rituals it was removed and placed in regular graves of the type mentioned above. These former graves remained open and thus the layers of sand and clay got deposited in them. An alternative guess may be that these graves were of a symbolic nature, associated with persons who may have died elsewhere and only the ritual was performed in these graves.

There was yet another variety at Kalibangan. The graves of this type were also located in the same general area, but a little away from the two groups just discussed. In this case the pit was circular or ovoid and not rectangular. Again, while there were plenty of pottery and toiletry objects including a mirror, no skeletal remains were found except for a fragmentary bone-piece in only one of the sixteen graves excavated of this type. It also needs to be added that these graves did not contain any bands of sand and clay as were encountered in the graves of the second type mentioned above, which would mean that these were not of the same category. Amongst the pottery, it was observed that there invariably was, almost as a central piece, a large globular pot (pl. VIIIB). It was thought for a while that it might contain charred bones/ ashes, implying a post-cremation burial, but no such evidence turned up. While these graves too seem to have a funerary association, their exact nature remains indeterminate, thus calling for further investigation.

The cemetery at Lothal presented yet another riddle. Out of the twenty graves excavated, all of which were of the extended-burial type, three produced two skeletons each (fig. 14.2). This naturally gave rise to a debate, namely whether these were examples of what is known in later-day India as the practice of *satī*, i.e. the wife immolating herself at the pyre of her husband. While this may be a tempting premise, the evidence of physical anthropology does not seem to uphold this view. Perhaps it may not be out of place to give to the reader a little bit of insight into this debate.

As elsewhere, at Lothal too, all the excavated graves were numbered. Thus, the graves having two skeletons each bore nos. 2, 7 and 11. Along with the skeletal remains from other graves, those from these graves were examined by two sets of experts. In respect of the skeletons from Graves 7 and 11, one of the experts (S.S. Sarkar in Rao 1985) stated that both the skeletons in these graves were those of males. However, about Grave 2 he opined that while one of the skeletons was that of a male the sex of the other could not be

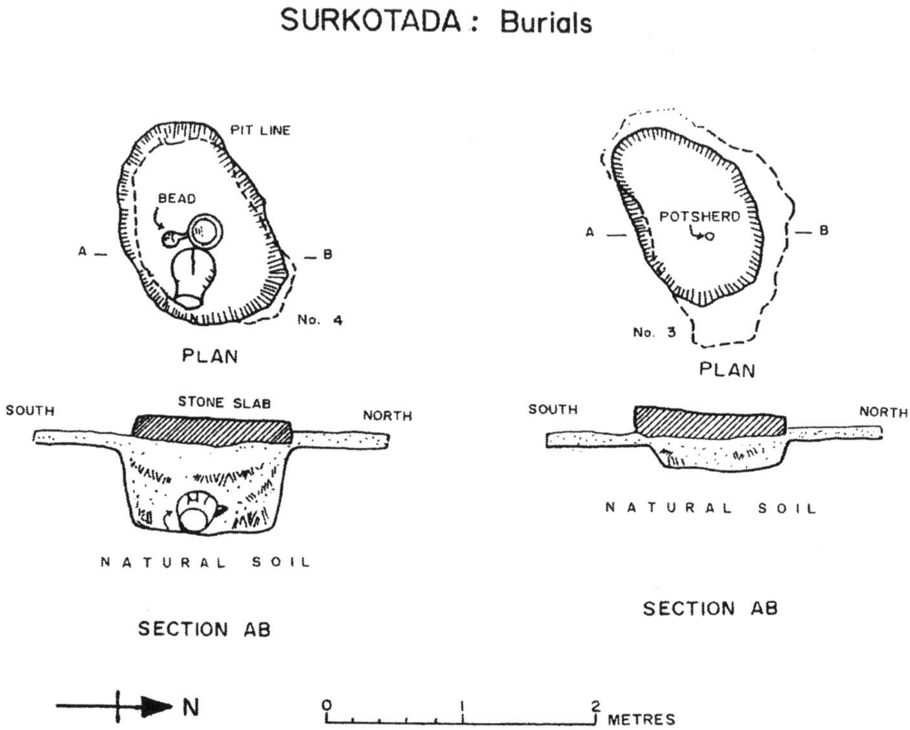

Fig. 14.3 Surkotada: Burials

determined. On the other hand, referring to the other set of experts, Rao (1979: 141) avers: 'In this connection it may be mentioned that according to Chatterjee and Kumar four skeletons from Lothal are said to be females. Two of them are from joint burials.' In view of these contradictory views of the experts, there is no way to resolve the issue. Perhaps the reader might like to say why not refer the matter to a third set of experts for adjudication!

Yet another surprise, this time from Surkotada. Of the four graves excavated here, none was of the usual extended burial type. On the contrary, these yielded only fragments of skeletal remains or even no bones at all. In one case, 'the pit yielded a red ware sherd of an urn and very small charred human bone splinters or remains' Joshi (1990: 369) then adds: 'The post-cremation human remains found in a burial bear a great significance. The relatives of the dead in all probability out of regard for the deceased used to take care of the burnt or charred bones after submission of the corpse to fire.'

A further noteworthy feature about the Surkotada burials is the use of stones for lining the graves. Often these were also covered with capstones and even had a scattering of stone-rubble over them (fig.14.3). The use of stones in the aforesaid manner reminds one of the megalithic graves of south India. However, it needs to be stated that whereas in the south Indian graves, the usual practice was first to expose the body to the elements and birds and then collect some bones and the skull and inter them in megalithic chambers, in the case of the Surkotada graves no such method seems to have been adopted. Further, the associated pottery in the megalithic graves is generally a black-and-red ware but this ware is nowhere to be found in the Surkotada graves. At the same time it must be recalled that in Subperiod IC at this site, a white-painted black-and-red ware had made its appearance and it is also known from evidence from other sites that in the course of time, the paintings gave way and only plain black-and-red ware continued. The question then is: Are we here on way to Megalithism?

This question repeats itself when we consider the burial evidence from Dholavira. Here, out of the many graves excavated, only one is of the standard Harappan type, i.e. having a full skeleton, laid supine in an extended position, with the head on the north. The remaining graves show two separate characteristics, viz. (i) 'megalithism'; and (ii) *stūpa*-like superstructure.

Of the first type at least two graves may be mentioned. In one case the grave-pit was rectangular, measuring 2.75 m x 1.35 m and oriented along the cardinal directions. It had no bones, but three pots. The megalithic element consisted of orthostats and an overlying stone cairn. The other grave, also rectangular (2.55 m x 1.70 m) and oriented north-south and east-west, had a clay 'coffin' in it but without any bones. There were, however, pots some of which were placed even below the 'coffin'. The grave was lined with vertical stones and seems to have had a capstone overlain by stone rubble.

No less interesting is a complex in the same cemetery area which has a *stūpa*-like superstructure, made of mud bricks. It has a diameter of about 35 m. and the extant height is approximately 2.5 m above the surrounding ground-level. The excavation of the *stūpa* is yet to be completed but, as of now, it appears to have had a solid mud-brick base with radial walls in the upper part. However, of the latter only one has been identified so far. If more are found, these might be construed as 'spokes', if the pattern of later-day *stūpas* is projected back. In the central part of this *stūpa* there is a vertical shaft, the bottom of which has not yet been reached. It is, therefore, not known if it contained any corporeal remains.

If we try to look for the 'origin' of these two concepts, viz. 'megalithism' and '*stūpa*-ism', we find that both are in a way rooted in the Harappan tradition. The provision of orthostats is just a replication of the mud-brick walls encountered in many of the 'standard' Harappan graves (see, for example, the grave from Kalibangan, fig. 14.1). In an area where stone is available in plenty and where the fortification walls and residential structures were made of stone, use of stone slabs for lining the graves is but natural. To come to the stone cairns, this also seems to be an extension of the Harappan tradition. During the course of his excavations at Harappa, Wheeler came across two cases in which there was evidence of a tumulus above the grave. While in one case it was just a pile of earthwork, in the other the superstructure was a regular construction of mud bricks (Wheeler 1947: pl. XXXVIIIA). In fact, in the photograph one may also observe that this tumulus is circular on plan. This example, thus, is not far removed from the *stūpa*-concept. For, after all, what is a *stūpa*, if not a superstructure built over the corporeal remains of the dead?

The skeletal remains sometimes throw very interesting sidelights too. For example, at Kalibangan a child had an unusually large head. It was evidently a case of excessive accumulation of water in the brain-cells which caused swelling and consequent enlargement of the head. To deal with the malady, the Kalibangan 'surgeons' trephined the head so that water could be drained out. This is indicated by three small holes in the right temporal region. A case of trephination has also been reported from Lothal. Once discovered, this kind of treatment was continued through the ages. There is literary evidence that trephination was practised by the renowned medical expert Jivaka who was a contemporary of the Buddha.

CHAPTER XV

THE TRUANT HORSE CLEARS THE HURDLES

Whether or not the horse was one of the animals known to the Harappans has long been a matter of debate. This debate has rather an ideological basis, since one of the agruments to disassociate the Harappans from the Indo-Aryans has been the supposed absence of the horse from the list of animals familiar to the former. And indeed if it was a fact that the Harappans did not know the horse, their claim for any kind of 'Aryanship' must fall to the ground, since right from the Rigvedic times the horse played an important role in the life of the Indo-Aryans. Anyway, while we shall discuss in a later chapter (XVII) the question regarding the Harappans vis-a-vis the Aryans, here we shall deal only with the association of the horse with the Harappan Civilization.

During the course of his excavations at Mohenjo-daro between 1927 and 1931, Mackay came across, amongst other terracotta models of animals, one example about which he stated (Mackay 1938, vol. I, p. 289; vol. II, pl. LXXVIII, 11): 'Perhaps the most interesting of the model animals is one that I personally take to represent a horse.' Dealing with this topic in 1968 Wheeler wrote (p. 92): 'One terracotta, from a late level of Mohenjo-daro [evidently referring to the specimen just mentioned], seems to represent a horse, reminding us that the jaw-bone of a horse is also recorded from the site, and that the horse was known at a considerably earlier period in northern Baluchistan.'

However, in spite of these categorical statements the horse remained a suspect. The reason seems to lie in the fact that whereas other animals like the bull, buffalo, goat, etc. were duly depicted on the seals, the horse was

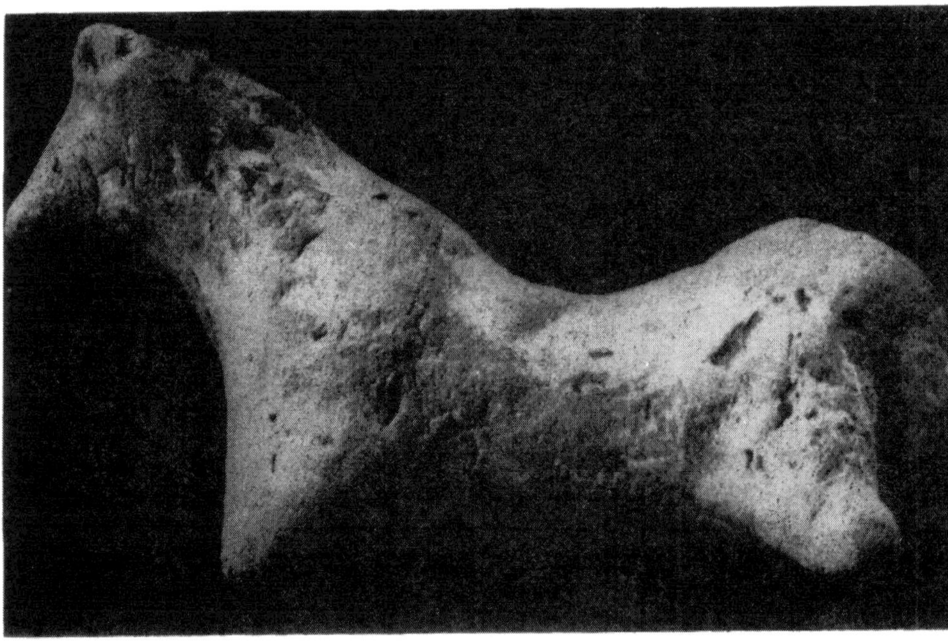

Fig. 15.1 Lothal: Terracotta horse

not. But then the same argument would apply to the camel which is also totally absent from the seals. However, camel's was not the bone of contention since it did not carry with it any ethnic insignia.

Anyway, the Indian excavations have amply proved that the horse was duly known to the Harappans. The evidence comes from Lothal, Surkotada, Kalibangan, etc. and because of the extreme significance of the debate we shall deal with it in some detail.

From Phase III (Period A) of Lothal, which is Mature Harappan, has been recovered a terracotta figurine of the horse (fig. 15.1). It has an elongated body with thick stumpy tail. A low ridge over the neck marks out the mane. And this terracotta figure is not the only evidence from Lothal. Amongst the faunal remains from the site is a second upper molar. Commenting on it, the experts, namely Bhola Nath, Zoologist, Zoological Survey of India, and G.V. Sreenivasa Rao of the Archaeological Survey of India, state (in S.R. Rao 1985, p. 641): 'The single tooth of the horse referred to above indicates the presence of the horse at Lothal during the Harappan period. The tooth from Lothal resembles closely with that of the modern horse and has pli-caballian (a minute fold near the base of the spur or protocone) which is well distinguishable character of the cheek teeth of the horse.'

Surkotada in Kachchha has yielded quite a few bones of the horse. These come from all the subperiods (IA, IB and IC) of the Harappan occupation (A.K. Sharma, in Joshi 1990: 381). The identification made by Sharma has been fully endorsed by Professor Sandor Bokonyi, Director of the Archaeological Institute, Budapest, Hungary, who is an internationally recognized archaeozoologist. In a letter dated 13 December 1993, addressed to the then Director General of the Archaeological Survey of india, he avers: 'Through a thorough study of the equid remains of the prehistoric settlement of Surkotada, Kachchha, excavated under the direction of Dr. J.P. Joshi, I can state the following: The occurrence of true horse (*Equus Caballus* L.) was evidenced by the enamel pattern of the upper and lower cheek and teeth and by the size and form of incisors and phalanges (toe bones). Since no wild horses lived in India in post-Pleistocene times, the domestic nature of the Surkotada horses is undoubtful. This is also supported by an intermaxilla fragment whose incisor tooth shows clear signs of crib biting, a bad habit only existing among domestic horses which are not extensively used for war.'

Up in the north, Rupnagar (formerly known as Ropar) and Kalibangan have also yielded remains of the horse. Kalibangan material includes an upper molar, a fragment of shaft of distal end of femur and the distal end of left humerus (Sharma 1993).

From Pakistan too, the evidence, though meagre, is in the positive. We have already referred to the terracotta figurine and jaw-bone of the horse from Mohenjo-daro. Although Vats and the current excavators of Harappa, Meadow and Kenoyer, have not reported any horse bones from the site, an ealier collection from there, sent to the Zoological Survey of India and examined by its specialist, Bhola Nath, did include remains of the horse. Even from a pre-Harappan site in Pakistan, viz. Rana Ghundai, Ross reported a few teeth of the horse, though Zeuner did not agree with the identification. However, the most startling discovery comes from the recent excavation at Nausharo, conducted by Jarrige et al. (in press). In the Harappan levels over here have been found clearly identifiable terracotta figurines of this animal.

Though no doubt one would always like to have more and more evidence, even the present evidence is sufficient to dispel any doubt about the association of the horse (*Equus Caballus* Linn.) with the Harappan Civilization. The truant horse has indeed crossed the hurdles!

CHAPTER XVI

CHRONOLOGICAL HORIZON OF THE HARAPPAN CIVILIZATION SECURELY FIXED

In his report on the excavations at Mohenjo-daro, Marshall assigned the Harappan Civilization to ca. 3250-2750 BC. This he did on the basis of the occurrence of certain objects of Harappan origin in Western Asia. Out of these, he wrote (Marshall 1931: 103-4): 'The most important are five seals of characteristic "Indus" pattern discovered at different sites in Elam and Mesopotamia, which in two cases at least must be definitely assigned to Pre-Sargonic Period and in no case can be referred to a later date than the third millennium BC. ... This is incontestable.' There, however, was a snag in this chronological equation, viz. from which horizon of Mohenjo-daro—Early, Intermediate or Late—did the seals found in Mesopotamia actually come? Thus Marshall himself added: 'Inasmuch, however, as there is at present no way of determining this point, we have assumed provisionally that the Ur and Kish [the sites concerned in Mesopotamia] seals belong to the Intermediate Period, and we have suggested accordingly that the occupation of Mohenjo-daro fell approximately between 3250 and 2750 BC.'

More views have been put forward since Marshall's days. According to one, this civilization fell between 2500 and 1500 BC, while another shortened its life-span and placed it within a tight jacket of 2300-2000 BC.

As seen above, Marshall had to depend for his dating on the evidence of contact of the Harappan Civilization with that in Western Asia. During his days there was no method of 'direct' dating. Strangely, coinciding with the decade of Indian Independence there came up a new technique of dating the

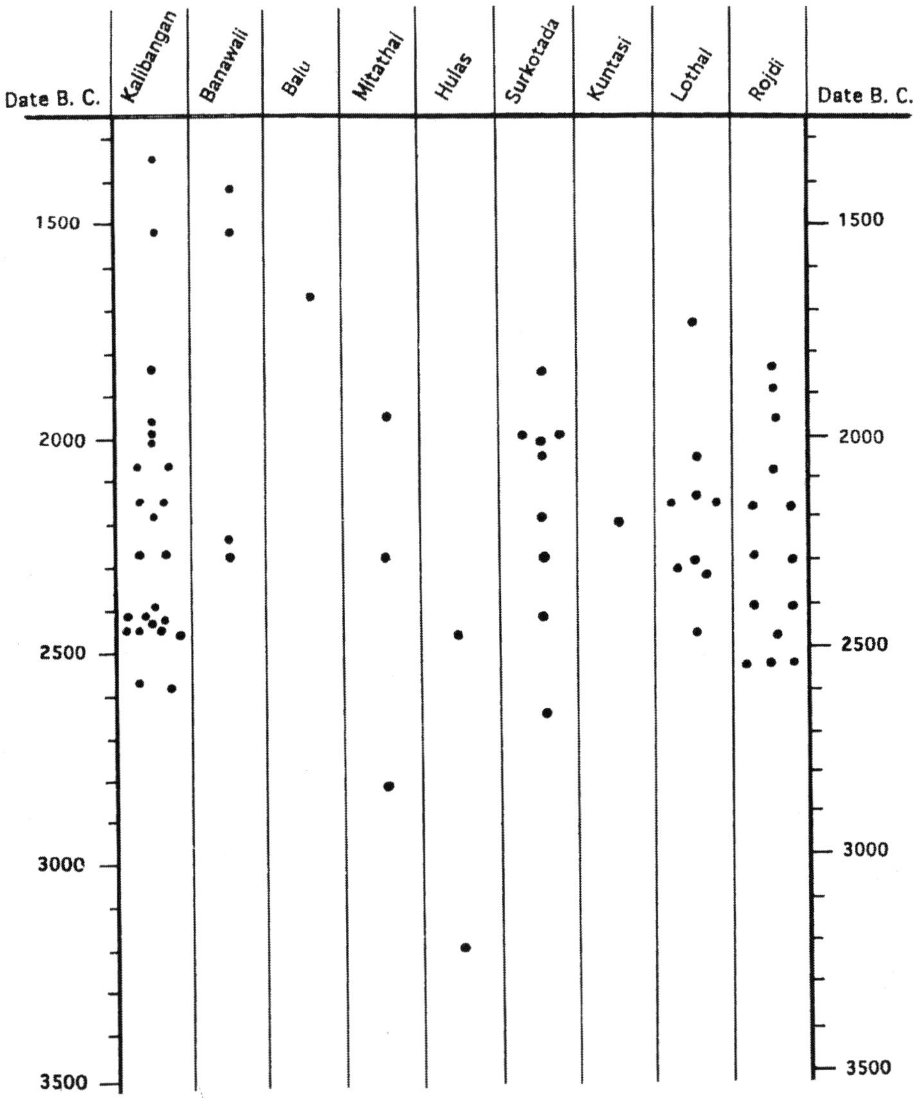

Fig. 16.1 Radiocarbon dates for the Mature Phase of the Harappan Civilization

past. It is known as the C-14 or radiocarbon method of dating. The method dates organic remains, such as charcoal, wood and bone recovered from an excavation. The dates assigned to these organic samples then become the dates of the stratum or deposit from which the samples are derived. If we have a number of samples from the various levels of a site, it becomes easier to assess the lifetime of the site.

At present two laboratories in India, namely the Physical Research Laboratory, Ahmedabad, and Birbal Sahni Institute of Palaeobotany, Lucknow, are engaged on dating archaeological samples by this technique. Samples are also sent now and then to laboratories outside the country. A large number of samples from various Harappan sites have been dated by this method and the same are plotted on a chart to give a visual picture (fig. 16.1). From the chart it would be seen that only two dates, one from Mitathal and the other from Hulas, pre-date 2700 BC. Further, only one date, from Surkotada, lies between 2700 and 2600 BC. There are at least five dates between 2600 and 2500 BC. From 2500 BC onwards there is a heavy concentration of dates. This concentration begins to peter out after 2000 BC. Later than 1800 BC the dates are very sporadic as was the case prior to 2600 BC. It would thus work out that the main lifespan of the Mature Phase of the Harappan Civilization was between 2600 and 2000 BC, with a margin of about a hundred years on the later side. The beginning of the Early Harappan Phase, as discussed in Chapter II, is ascribable to the first quarter of the third millennium BC. As to the Late Harappan Phase, it may have persisted for a couple of hundred years after 1900 BC.

CHAPTER XVII

THE MYTH OF ARYAN INVASION: REFLECTIONS ON THE AUTHORSHIP OF THE HARAPPAN CIVILIZATION

Ever since the discovery of the Harappan Civilization in the early 1920s, one of the most debated issues has been its authorship. Both Marshall and Mackay, the excavators of Mohenjo-daro, held that the Dravidians must have been its authors, though they had no clinching evidence to that effect. They seem to have had at the back of their minds a nineteenth century thesis, propounded by Max Muller, according to which the *Veda*s were unlikely to have been earlier than ca. 1200 BC. Since the Harappan Civilization had come to an end well before that date, it was but tempting for them to have argued that the Harappan Civilization was pre-Vedic and hence pre- and non-Aryan. A non-Aryan candidate most easily available to them was the Dravidian and hence the theory that the Harappans were Dravidians. (At that point of time, the terms 'Dravidian' and 'Aryan' were used in a racial sense, but now these have acquired a linguistic connotation.)

This theory was given a shot in the arm by Mortimer Wheeler in the 1940s. While reporting on his excavations at Harappa (Wheeler 1947: 82), he pronounced the verdict: 'On circumstantial evidence Indra stands accused.' In this judgement, Indra, standing for the Aryans whose cherished god he was, was held responsible for the destruction of the fort unearthed by Wheeler at Harappa. Though there was no evidence of any wanton destruction of the fort at Harappa, yet the temptation to hold Indra responsible for the supposed destruction came from a word, '*puraṁdara*,' occurring in the

Vedic texts, which means 'destroyer of forts.' The logic was simplistic.

To give legitimacy to his thesis, Wheeler referred to the skeletal remains found at Mohenjo-daro and declared that here lay the people massacred by the invading Aryans. This alleged massacre has been examined by a number of scholars (e.g. Dales 1964) and it has been demonstrated that there is no case whatsoever for such an assumption. In the first place, the skeletons were encountered in different stratigraphic levels. Had the persons concerned died as a result of an attack by some invaders and the site had to be abandoned, the skeletons would have come from a single level—which would have been the uppermost—and not from different ones. Secondly, some of the skeletons bore cut-marks that had been healed. Had the death been the result of a massacre involving immediate death, the wounds would have had no time to heal. Lastly, one does expect some material remains at the site associated with the invaders. But no such remains were found. The Jhukar pottery that occurs in the upper levels at Mohenjo-daro has been shown to represent a devolution from the Harappan pottery itself rather than being alien (Mughal 1992). Dales has very rightly pronounced a counter verdict, dubbing this as 'mythical massacre'.

In final analysis, therefore, Indra must be exonerated from the charges of having massacred the Mohenjo-darians and having destroyed the Harappan forts.

But all this is no answer to our initial enquiry about the authorship of this great civilization of South Asia. If the Aryans were not its destroyers, it does not automatically follow that they were its creators. The issue has to be examined in greater depth.

As of now, scholars have put up the candidature of the Dravidian-speaking people on the one hand and of the Sanskrit-speaking people on the other. The more noteworthy amongst the Dravidianists are Asko Parpola et al. (1969) and W.A. Fairservis (1992). Amongsts the Sanskritists, particular mention may be made of S.R. Rao (1982), M.V.N. Krishna Rao (1982) and Richter-Ushanas (1992). The last one has even read whole verses from the *Ṛigveda* in the inscriptions on some of the seals. The author has reviewed the theses of most of these decipherers and has shown that not only are their results untenable but also the methodology (cf. Lal 1970, 1974, 1983; also Possehl 1996). The interesting point is that, amongst themselves, not even two Dravidianists nor two Sanskritists arrive at the same readings. It is thus abundantly clear that the most dependable key to unlock the authorship mystery, viz. the identification of the Harappan language, has not yet been found.

And yet the controversy goes on. Perhaps the reader might like to know some of the other arguments adduced in support of the above-mentioned two theses.

To take up the Dravidian hypothesis first. It may be recalled that the Dravidian theory rests on the assumption that since the Harappan Civilization was destroyed by the Aryans they cannot be its authors. And since there are only two major linguistic groups in India, viz. the Indo-Aryan and the Dravidian, the Harappans must have belonged to the latter.

One argument is the presence of a pocket of Brahui-speaking people in a part of Baluchistan. It has been argued that Brahui is related to the Dravidian group of languages and when the Dravidian-speaking Harappans were pushed southward by the invading Indo-Aryans, a small group managed to stay on in this little enclave. The flaws in this argument are many. In the first place, there is a debate even about the very affiliation of Brahui with the Dravidian group. Some scholars are even of the view that it is more akin to 'modern colloquial eastern Elamite.' Some others opine that these Brahui-speaking people in a pocket of Baluchistan are not the original inhabitants of the area but migrated there during the medieval times.

Another argument that militates against the theory that the Dravidian-speaking Harappans were pushed down all the way to southern India by the invading Aryans is that in **none** of the areas where a Dravidian language—Tamil, Telugu, Kannada or Malayalam—is spoken is there **any trace whatsoever** of the material remains of the Harappan Civilization. The only archaeological remains of a comparable antiquity in these areas are those of the Southern Neolithic Culture. Is one then to believe that the Harappans reverted overnight from a full-fledged Bronze Age to a Neolithic one?

Secondly, if the Dravidian language was really spoken during the Harappan times in Pakistan and in Rajasthan, Haryana, Panjab and northern parts of Uttar Pradesh, one does expect that at least a few Dravidian names of places, rivers, mountains, etc. would have survived in these areas. But this is not the case at all. Such a continuity of names of an earlier language have been noticed the world over where a later language has overridden the earlier one. Europe has many examples to offer of names in an earlier language even after the introduction of a later one. Likewise, many of the American Indian names continue to exist in the United States of America even after its colonization by Europeans.

There is yet another argument that is advanced to support the Harappan-Dravidian equation. This relates to the occurrence of some Dravidian words in the Vedic language. According to this line of argument, the Indo-Aryan conquerors picked up certain words from the conquered Harappans. While there may well be a few words of Dravidian origin in early Sanskrit, the foregoing is not the only way in which this limited Dravidian-to-Sanskrit borrowing can be explained. If, just for argument's sake, it is assumed that the Harappans spoke Sanskrit, they could have easily borrowed the Dravidian words from their contemporaries in the south, viz. the Southern Neolithic people, who, logic suggests, are likely to have spoken a Dravidian tongue. Ever since the dawn of history we have no evidence of any language other than a Dravidian one having been spoken in that region.

However, even after demonstrating that the Indo-Aryans were not the destroyers of the Harappan Civilization and also after showing that all the arguments advanced in favour of the Harappans having spoken a Dravidian language are untenable, we still remain in square one, since we have so far not achieved any positive results. We may now consider arguments against and in favour of the Indo-Aryans having been the authors of the Harappan Civilization.

The greatest mental barrier that was ever erected against even a remote thought that the Harappans could have been the Indo-Aryans was the fatwa given by Max Muller in the nineteenth century, namely that the *Ṛigveda* was unlikely to have been earlier than ca. 1200 BC. Although later on the clergy himself (Muller 1890, reprint 1979) backed out by saying, 'Whether the Vedic hymns were composed in 1000, or 1500, or 2000, or 3000 BC, no power on earth will ever determine,' his followers even today tenaciously adhere to the fatwa. According to these scholars, therefore, there is no chance of the Indo-Aryans having been the authors of the Harappan Civilization, since it well predated the *Lakṣmaṇa rekhā* * of 1200 BC.

Anyway, we must re-examine briefly the various data regarding the dating of the Vedic texts. An evidence often quoted by astronomers is the mention in the *Aitareya Brāhmaṇa* of the shifting of the vernal equinox from the *Nakṣatra* Mṛigaśiras to Rohiṇī. According to these astronomers, this event is likely to have taken place about 3500 BC. With this as the date for the *Aitareya Brāhmaṇa*, the *Ṛigveda* is bound to be still earlier. This is an important piece of evidence which should not be brushed aside. It needs to be examined by a body of international experts.

In so far as archaeology is concerned, it does not carry us back that far, though certainly much before the *Lakṣmaṇa rekhā* of 1200 BC. The well-known inscription from Boghaz Keui in West Asia refers to a treaty between a Hittite king Suppiluliuma and a Mitanni king Matiwaza. Herein four Vedic gods, viz. Indra, Mitra, Nāsatya and Varuṇa are invoked as witnesses. The inscription is datable to the fourteenth century BC. In the archives of the Hittite capital has also been found a treatise which deals with horse-training and uses terms like *ekavartana, trivartana, pañchavartana*, which are characteristically Sanskritic. Further, referring to some of the other documents from West Asia, the famous scholar T. Burrow (1955: 29) opines: 'The Aryans appear in Mitanni from 1500 BC as the ruling dynasty, which means that they must first have entered the

* This is a reference to the Rāmāyana story. During the course of their exile, Rāma, Sītā and Lakṣmaṇa once stayed in a hut at Pañchavatī. Under a game-plan drawn up by Rāvaṇa, his brother Mārīchi appeared in front of the hut in the form of a golden deer. Attracted by it, Sītā asked Rāma to get her the deer and Rāma went out chasing it. When some distress signals were received, Sītā implored Lakṣmaṇa to go and help Rāma out. Sensing mischief that all this was being enacted by the Rākṣasas to abduct Sītā, Lakṣmaṇa drew a line in front of the door of the hut and asked Sītā never to cross it. Sītā ignored the advice and as soon as she crossed it, she was abducted by Rāvaṇa. This kind of line has come to be known as the *Lakṣmaṇa rekhā*, i.e. a line that must not be crossed, and if one does cross it, one is bound to be in trouble.

country as conquerors.' Conquerors from where? Around 1500 BC there was no other region where the above-mentioned gods were worshipped, except the Indian subcontinent. The inference, therefore, is self-evident. Thus, the Ṛigvedic Aryans are much anterior to 1500 BC.

At this point another piece of evidence needs to be brought into the picture. The *Ṛigveda* refers to the Sarasvatī as a mighty river, flowing from the mountains to the sea (cf. Misra 1994). The river, however, dried up before the Mahābhārata times, according to the textual data. Archaeological evidence from Kalibangan, which stood on the bank of the Sarasvatī, indicates that the site was abandoned because of the drying up of that river. According to radiocarbon dates, this abandonment took place around 1900 BC (Lal 1997: 245 and 263). Thus, putting the literary and archaeological evidence together, it follows that the ***Ṛigveda* must antedate 1900 BC**, namely the time by which the Sarasvatī dried up.

Attention must be drawn to a piece of collateral evidence. In a recent paper Hemphill et al. (1991) affirm as follows: 'As foı the question of biological continuity within the Indus Valley, two discontinuities appear to exist. The first occurs between 6000 and 4500 BC and is reflected by the strong separation in dental non-metric characters between neolithic and chalcolithic burials at Mehrgarh. The second occurs at some point after 800 BC but before 200 BC. In the intervening period, while there is dental non-metric, craniometric, and cranial non-metric evidence for a degree of an internal biological continuity, statistical evaluation of cranial data reveals clear indication of interaction with the West specifically with the Iranian Plateau.'

From the foregoing data it is clear that there was a basic biological continuity from ca. 4500 BC to ca. 800 BC. If that be so, where is the possibility of the much-advertised large-scale immigration of the supposedly non-Harappan and alien Indo-Aryans around 1500 BC? Could these chalcolithic people, who later gave rise to the Harappan Civilization, themselves have been the ancestors of the Vedic Aryans? These chalcolithic people had certain things in common with the chalcolithic people of Afghanistan, north-eastern Iran and southern parts of Central Asia. It is thus most likely that the north-western part of the Indian subcontinent, together with the aforesaid region, may have been the 'original home' of the Aryans.

The Vedic geography must also set us re-thinking in this context. While on the east the Ṛigvedic people were familiar with the upper reaches of the Gaṅgā and Yamunā, in the west they refer to the Kubhā, Krumu and Gomatī, which are the present-day Kabul, Kurram and Gomal rivers of Afghanistan and north-western Pakistan. In between, of course, the Indus and its tributaries are duly mentioned as also the Sarasvatī, a river so highly eulogized in the *Vedas*. This is precisely the area in which the Harappan Civilization flourished.

An argument that has often been advanced against an Indo-Aryan-Harappan equation is that whereas the Harappan Civilization was urban in character, the cultural milieu of the *Vedas* was essentially rural. So how can the two be equated? This notion is highly mistaken and here is some evidence which categorically counters the same.

It has been orchestrated that the Aryans were nomads or at best lived in villages and knew no cities. The word *pur* occurring in the *Ṛigveda* has often been misinterpreted. According to Macdonell and Keith (1912, reprint 1982, Vol. I: 538), it means a 'fort', 'rampart' or 'stronghold'. In this context it may be well worthwhile to quote a verse from the *Ṛigveda* itself:

...varma sīvyadhvam bahulā pṛithūni
puraḥ kṛiṇudhvamāyasīradhṛiṣṭā (ṚV X. 101. 8).

The verse is translated by Griffith (1973, reprint: 615) as follows:

'... stitch ye [oh god] the coats of armour, wide and many; make iron forts, secure from all assailants'.

In earlier Vedic texts the word '*ayas*' meant 'metal' in general, and it was only later that two separate words came to be used, viz. *kṛiṣṇāyas* and *lohāyas* meaning respectively black metal i.e. iron and red metal i.e. copper. Anyway, in the verse cited above, the prayer was for the construction of a very strong fort so that it was not vulnerable. The texts even refer to forts with a hundred arms (*śatabhujī*), which implies settlements with multiple fortifications such as found at Dholavira.

On the economic front too, the Vedic Aryans were very well off. They were engaged even in sea-trade, for which they used boats with a hundred (i.e. a large number of) oars (*śatāritra*). A verse from the Ṛigveda (IX. 33. 6) goes:

> *rāyaḥ samudrānśchaturo asmabhyam soma viśvataḥ; ā pavasa sahasriṇaḥ.*
>
> 'From every side, o Soma, for our profit, pour thou forth four seas filled full [sic] of riches thousandfold.' (Griffith 1973, reprint: 483).

There are many other verses in the Vedic texts which clearly show that, like that of the 'Aryan invasion,' it is yet another myth that the Aryans had nothing to do with urban life. (For more details see Singh 1995.) It has to be realized that, in the first place, the Vedic texts were religious in character and thus had only a limited field and were in no case a charter on urban life. Secondly, it has also to be realized that at all times in history and in all countries of the world there have been both the components—rural as well as urban. So why should the Vedic texts not reflect the rural component as well? Anyway, what do we do with terms like *rājan, samrāṭ, janarāj, rāṣṭra, samiti, sabhā, adhyakṣa,* etc. occurring in the Vedic texts, which clearly refer to categories of rulers, assemblies, etc?

Another, and very legitimate, objection against the association of the Harappan Civilization with the Indo-Aryans has been the alleged absence of the horse from this civilization. As discussed in Chapter XV, this is again proving to be a make-belief.

Thus, like the pins in bowling, the various objections against a Harappan–Indo-Aryan equation are falling off. But let us remember that the setting aside of such objections is not the way to prove the case. It can at best be evidence of a circumstantial kind. Positive proof has yet to come.

The reader may perhaps feel disappointed that the author has not made any categorical statement either way. Unfortunately, this is so. All that can be said at the moment is that: (i) there is no clinching evidence whatsoever to establish the much advertised equation that the Harappans were a Dravidian-speaking people; (ii) the Indo-Aryan authorship of the Harappan Civilization cannot be ruled out, but is not yet categorically proved; and (iii) the final verdict can come only when the Harappan script is **really** deciphered. Let us hope that that day is not far off.

CHAPTER XVIII

LOOKING AHEAD

While the readers might like to congratulate Indian archaeologists on what they have achieved during the fifty years since Independence, the archaeologists on their part are fully conscious of:

What has been done is but a part
of what remains, things all apart.
Let not a praise then make us burst,
Complacency the spade nor rust.

The first and foremost need is to speed up reports on the remaining excavations carried out at Harappan sites in the country since Independence. (A report on Kalibangan is also due from the author and his colleagues who jointly excavated the site. The author would not like to dilate on the sordid story of the delay, but would only state that, if all goes well, the first volume of the report, dealing with the Early Harappan Period, would be handed over for publication in the near future.) Indeed, the need is for the administrative auhorities as well as the excavators to put their heads together to remove all bottle-necks, so that reports see the light of the day as early as possible.

The second point relates to the planning of future fieldwork. Dholavira is one of the most important sites of the Harappan Civilization in India. Excavations over here are underway and while many new things have turned up, many questions yet remain to be answered by the site. The spade, therefore, must not rust. Another important site which is crying for investigation is Rakhigarhi in Haryana. It is being encroached upon fast and something has got to be done about it before it is too late.

Kunal in Haryana has thrown very valuable light on what has come to be known as the Early or Formative Stage of the Harappan Civilization. In the first place, all possible assistance should be provided to the excavators to finalize the report and publish it. Secondly, a few more sites of similar vintage must be explored and excavated so that a fuller picture of the evolution of the Harappan Civilization, from its Early to the Mature Stage, is obtained. For all one knows, explorations might also reveal a stage anterior to that of Kunal.

We have stated earlier that, in spite of tall claims, the Harappan script still remains to be deciphered. Amongst other reasons for this failure may be the fact that each decipherer tends to live in his own world of imagination, little bothering about the basics of methodology and about checks and balances. To begin with, what is needed is a dialogue, a long-drawn dialogue verging on debate, amongst the proponents of the various decipherments, so that each one gets to know where he has gone astray. Thus, many untenable theses will get dropped.

However, that is only one part of the approach. The real thing is to bring together, on the one hand, such decipherers as are able to shed off their pre-conceived notions and are willing to start afresh and, on the other, specialists in linguistics and Dravidian and Sanskrit languages and even those who are professionals in decoding. Such a group or groups must meet and discuss various possibilities and carve out their own path ahead. Group-work seems to be the need of the hour and it is in this task that the Archaeological Survey of India and institutions engaged in linguistic studies must take the initiative. No ego should come in the way and no expenditure should be regarded too much on this collaborative project. On the occasion of the Golden Jubilee of India's Independence, will Government of India rise to the occasion? May it be hoped that this appeal does not remain a cry in the wilderness, even though in the past many have had that unfortunate fate.

COLOUR PLATES

Pl. IA. Kunal: Early Harappan pottery

Pl. IB. Kunal: Spiralled bangles, silver, Early Harappan

Pl. IC. Mohenjo-daro: Dancing girl wearing spiralled bangles, bronze, Mature Harappan

Pl. IIA. Kunal: Silver ornaments, Early Harappan

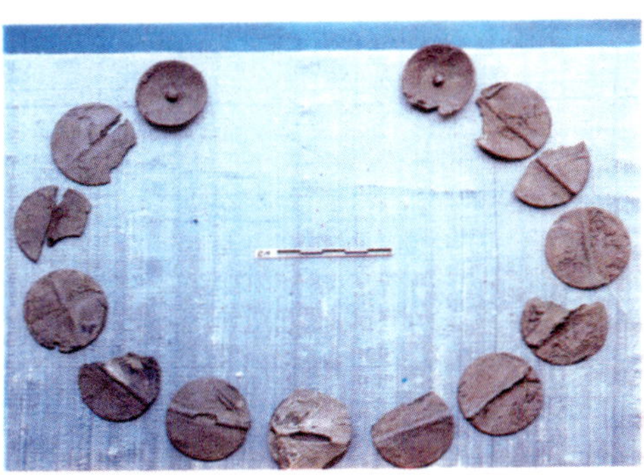

Pl. IIB. Kunal: Discular beads of silver, with axial perforation, Early Harappan

Pl. IIC. Lothal: Discular beads of gold, with axial perforation, Mature Harappan

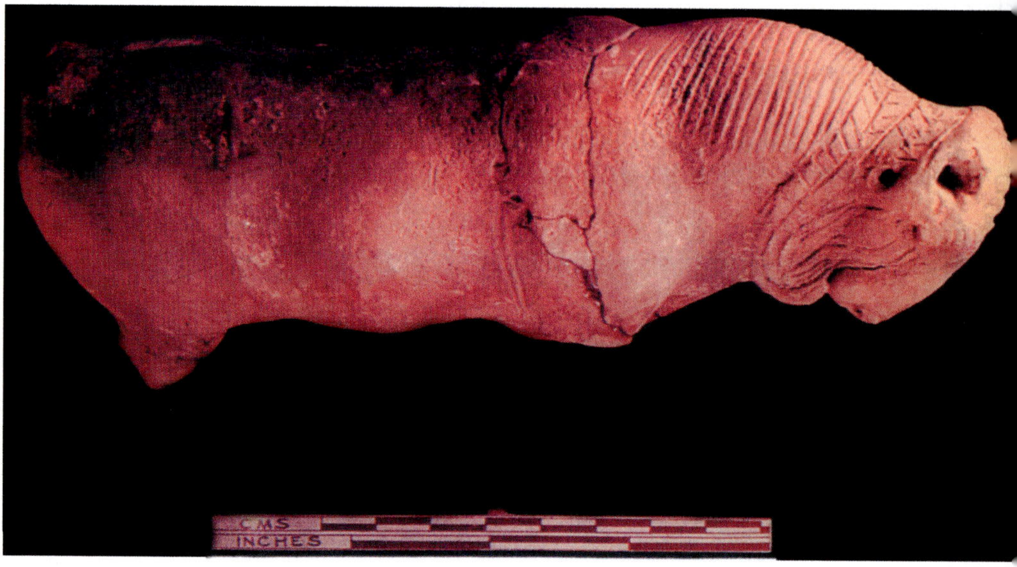

Pl. IIIA. Kalibangan: Terracotta bull, Mature Harappan

Pl. IIIB. Kalibangan: Bronze bull, Mature Harappan

Pl. IVA. Kalibangan: Cylinder seal and its impression, Mature Harappan

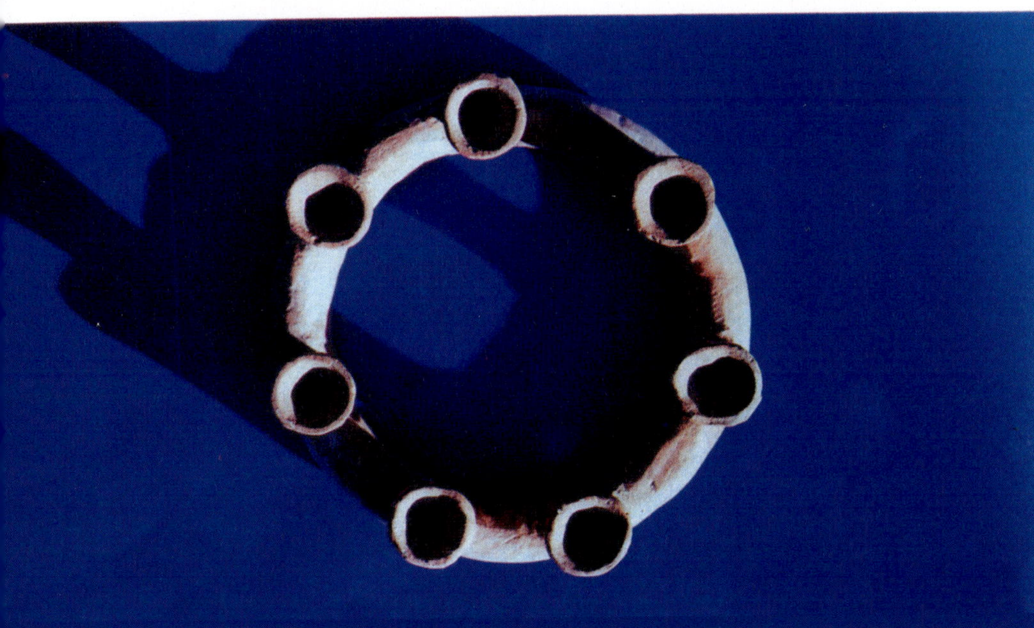

l. IVB. Kalibangan: Terracotta *kernos*, Mature Harappan

Pl. VA. Daimabad: Copper buffalo

Pl. VB. Daimabad: Copper chariot

Pl. VIA. Dholavira: A well in the Castle. The lines on the edge of the horizontal slab of the trough were produced by the rope that constantly passed over it in the process of drawing water

Pl. VIB. Dholavira: A sketch to illustrate how water was drawn from the well. Prior to the recent introduction of electrically operated tube-wells, the same method was followed in villages

Pl. VIIA. Dholavira: A wall of the water-reservoir, south of the Castle. Mark the faces of the stones, which were dressed with bronze tools. Iron was not known then

VIIB. Dholavira: A sketch to illustrate how a nearby seasonal nullah, Manhar, was dammed and water brought to the reservoir

Pl. VIIIA. Dholavira: Stone pillars, unique in Harappan architecture

Pl. VIIIB. Kalibangan: Burial with pottery, but without skeletal remains, Harappan

BIBLIOGRAPHY

Agrawal, D.P. 1982. *The Archaeology of India*. Scandinavian Institute of Asian Studies Monograph Series, no. 46. London: Curzon Press.

Allchin, B. and F.R. Allchin. 1982. *The Rise of Civilization in India and Pakistan*. Cambridge: Cambridge University Press.

Bisht, R.S. 1982. Excavations at Banawali: 1974-77. In G.L. Possehl (ed.), *Harappan Civilization: A Contemporary Perspective*, pp.113-24. New Delhi: Oxford and IBH Publishing Co.

—— 1989. A New Model of the Harappan Town Planning as Revealed at Dholavira in Kutch: A Surface Study of its Plan and Architecture. In B. Chatterji (ed.), *History and Archaeology*, pp. 397-408. Delhi: Ramanand Vidya Bhavan.

—— 1991. Dholavira: New Horizons of the Indus Civilization. *Puratattva*, 20:71-82.

—— 1994. Banawali. In J.P. Joshi and R.S. Bisht, *India and the Indus Civilization*, pp. 23-31. New Delhi.

Burrow, T. 1955. *The Sanskrit Language*. London: Faber and Faber.

Dales, G.F. 1964. The Mythical Massacre at Mohenjo-daro. *Expedition*, 6(3): 36-43.

Dhavalikar, M.K., M.R. Rawal and Y.M. Chitalwala. 1996. *Kuntasi: A Harappan Emporium on West Coast*. Pune: Deccan College Post-Graduate Research Institute.

Dikshit, K.N. 1982. Hulas and the Late Harappan Complex in Western Uttar Pradesh. In G.L. Possehl (ed.), *Harappan Civilization: A Contemporary Perspective*, pp. 339-51. New Delhi: Oxford and IBH Publishing Co.

Fairservis, W.A., 1992. *The Harappan Civilization and its Writing*. New Delhi: Oxford and IBH Publishing Co.

Griffith, R.T.H. 1973 [Reprint]. *The Hymns of the Rigveda*. Delhi: Motilal Banarsidass.

Gupta, S.P. 1996. *The Indus-Saraswati Civilization: Origins, Problems and Issues*. Delhi: Pratibha Prakashan.

Hemphill. B.E., J.R. Lukacs and K.A.R. Kennedy. 1991. Biological Adaptations and Affinities of Bronze Age Harappans. In R.H. Meadow (ed.), *Harappa Excavation 1986-1990*, pp. 137-82. Madison, Wisconsin: Prehistory Press.

Jarrige, J.-F. et al. (In press). *Excavations at Mehrgarh-Nausharo, 16th to 20th Seasons (1990-94)*. Report submitted to Director General of Archaeology and Museums, Government of Pakistan (unpublished, but privately circulated).

Joshi, J.P. 1990. *Excavation at Surkotada 1971-72 and Exploration in Kutch*. New Delhi: Archaeological Survey of India.

Joshi, J.P., Madhu Bala and Jassu Ram. 1984, The Indus Civilization: A Reconsideration on the Basis of Distribution maps. In B.B. Lal, S.P. Gupta, and Shashi Asthana (eds.), *Frontiers of the Indus Civilization*, pp. 511-30, New Delhi: Books and Books.

Khatri, J.S. and M. Acharya. 1995. Kunal: A New Indus-Saraswatī Site. *Puratattva*, 25:84-86.

Lal, B.B. 1966. The Direction of Writing in the Harappan Script. *Antiquity*, XL (157): 52-55.

——1970. Some Observations on the Harappan Script. In L. Chandra et al. (eds.), *India's Contribution to World Thought and Culture*, pp. 189-202, Madras.

—— 1970-71. Perhaps the Earliest Ploughed Field so far Excavated Anywhere in the World. *Puratattva*, 4:1-3.

Lal, B.B. 1974. *Has the Indus Script been Deciphered? An Assessment of Two Latest Claims*. Shimla: Indian Institute of Advanced Study.

—— 1979. Kalibangan and the Indus Civilization. In D.P. Agrawal and D.K. Chakrabarti (eds.), *Essays in Indian Protohistory*, pp. 65-97. New Delhi: B.R. Publishing Corporation.

—— 1983. Reading the Indus Script. *Indian and Foreign Review*, 20 (13): 33-36.

—— 1984. The Earliest Datable Earthquake in India. *Science Age* (October 1984), pp. 8-9. Bombay: Nehru Centre.

—— 1997. *The Earliest Civilization of South Asia*. New Delhi: Aryan Books International.

Macdonell, A.A. and A.B. Keith. 1982 (Reprint). *Vedic Index of Names and Subjects*. 2 vols. Delhi: Motilal Banarsidass.

Mackay, E.J.H. 1938. *Further Excavations at Mohenjo-daro*. 2 vols. Delhi: Government of India.

Marshall, J. 1931. *Mohenjo-daro and the Indus Civilization*. 3 vols. London: Arthur Probsthain.

Misra, V.N. 1994. Indus Civilization and the Ṛigvedic Sarasvatī. In Asko Parpola et al. (eds.), *South Asian Archaeology 1973*, pp. 511-25. Helsinki.

Mughal, M.R. 1992. Jhukar and Late Harappan Cultural Mosaic of the Greater Indus Valley. In C. Jarrige (ed.), *South Asian Archaeology 1989*, pp. 213-21. Madison, Wisconsin: Prehistory Press.

Muller, F.M. 1979 [Reprint]. *Physical Religion*. New Delhi: Asian Educational Services.

Parpola, A., S. Koskenniemi, S. Parpola and P. Aalto 1969. *Decipherment of the Proto-Dravidian Inscriptions of the Indus Civilization*. Copenhagen.

Possehl, G.L. 1996. *Indus Age: The Writing System*. New Delhi: Oxford and IBH Publishing Co. Pvt. Ltd.

Possehl, G.L. and C.F. Herman. 1990. The Sorath Harappan: A New Regional Manifestation of the Indus Urban Phase. In M. Taddei (ed.), *South Asian Archaeology 1987*, pp. 295-319.

Rao, M.V.N. Krishna., 1982. *Indus Script Deciphered*. Delhi: Agam Kala Prakashan.

Rao, S.R. 1962-63. Excavation at Rangpur and Other Explorations in Gujarat. *Ancient India*, 18-19:5-207.

—— 1979. *Lothal—A Harappan Port Town (1955-62)*, Vol. I. New Delhi: Archaeological Survey of India.

—— 1982. *The Decipherment of the Indus Script*. Bombay: Asia Publishing House.

—— 1985. *Lothal—A Harappan Port Town (1955-62)*. Vol. II. New Delhi: Archaeological Survey of India.

Richter-Ushanas, E. 1992. *The Fifth Veda: The Indus Seals in Comparison with the Ṛigveda*. Germany.

Sali, S.A. 1986. *Daimabad 1976-79*. New Delhi: Archaeological Survey of India.

Sharma, A.K. 1993. The Harappan Horse was buried under Dune of..., *Puratattva*, 23:30-34.

Sharma, Y.D. 1982. Harappan Complex on the Sutlej (India). In G.L. Possehl (ed.) *Harappan Civilization: A Contemporary Perspective*, pp. 141-65. New Delhi: Oxford and IBH Publishing Co.

Singh, Bhagwan. 1995. *The Vedic Harappans*. New Delhi: Aditya Prakashan.

Srivastava, K.M. 1991. *Madinat Hamad: Burial Mounds 1984-85*. Bahrain National Museum.

Vats, M.S. 1940. *Excavations at Harappa*. Delhi: Government of India. 2 vols.

Wheeler, R.E.M. 1947. Harappa 1946: The Defences and Cemetery R37. *Ancient India*, 3:58-130.

—— 1968. *The Indus Civilization*. 3rd edn. Cambridge: University Press.

INDEX